THE KEYS
to the Classroom

A basic manual
to help new language teachers find their way
SECOND EDITION

LESLIE BALDWIN

First Edition Author:
PAULA PATRICK

ACTFL
1001 North Fairfax Street, Suite 200
Alexandria, VA 22314

Graphic Design by Goulah Design Group, Inc.
Copy Editing by Todd Larson

ISBN: 978-1-942544-69-2

Foreword

"Why didn't anyone ever teach me about this in my methods course?" If you're a new teacher, you may have asked yourself that question a dozen times. The probable answer is that a methods course has so much to learn that your professors likely just couldn't fit it all in.

The truth is that surviving your first year(s) of teaching includes all of the important things you learned in your teacher preparation program, plus a whole lot more—things you'll learn on the job from colleagues, your school, and simply trial and error.

ACTFL has produced this handbook to help you avoid the trials of the errors as much as possible. In the pages that follow, you will find exceedingly important tips that will prepare you for opening day. You'll find ways to make it through those first challenging weeks when everything is new and you're establishing a sense of comfort and familiarity. And, as those weeks pass, you'll find yourself turning back to this guide as you prepare for Back-to-School Night, parent conferences, grading, and eventually those closing weeks of school. In just a few years, you'll be the one passing on the sage advice you'll find in this handbook, as you become the veteran expert helping to support the novice teachers in your school. But don't give the handbook away! You'll find yourself turning back to it time and again because of all of the good ideas that can help a good teacher become a great one.

Teaching is hard work. But then, anything worth doing usually is. The rewards of teaching are endless, and the chance to make a difference in the lives of students, in the future of your community, and in a global community far exceeds the dollars you'll earn. Never forget that good teaching matters—and the work you do matters more than ever.

All of us, members of ACTFL and veterans in the language teaching profession, are rooting for you. We hope that you will experience extraordinary successes, reap quiet rewards, and teach students who remind you every day that they are what it's all about.

Good luck!

Myriam Met
Independent Consultant

Dedication

To the beginning teachers who shared
their fears, frustrations, creative ideas, and
solutions; and to my colleagues, who are
dedicated to providing quality education
to America's future.

Introduction – *First Edition*

The teaching profession touches so many lives, and teachers have such a significant impact on students. Therefore, if asked to reflect on one's educational experience, most people could cite a teacher who made a difference for them. Now you have the opportunity to be one of those teachers. As a beginning language teacher, proficient in your subject matter but not necessarily well-versed in teaching methodology, you will be given a curriculum framework, basic rules and policies, some basic training, and a welcome to the field of teaching. You will also have lots of questions. Don't worry—we have lots of answers for you.

This handbook is designed to prepare new teachers—in short order—to tackle their first teaching assignment. You probably remember some of the savvy techniques with which your instructors in high school and college engaged you in the learning process and excited you about learning languages. And we'll review the best of them in the chapters to come. You'll also find lots of tips for setting up your classroom, establishing your grading process, creating an exciting learning environment, and figuring out how to meet your school and district curriculum requirements. We've included many templates you can use as-is or modify and revise as you wish. They will save you from reinventing the wheel in the process of establishing yourself as a teacher in your school.

A significant number of teachers—relative rookies as well as wise veterans, plus conference attendees and presenters, specialists, supervisors, and school administrators—contributed to the content of this handbook. You can benefit from their countless hours of classroom teaching, observations, debriefing sessions, teacher workshops, collaboration opportunities, and interventions over many years. We hope this handbook will give you a quick start in getting your classroom teaching career up and running.

Paula Patrick
Coordinator of World Languages, 2003-2012
Fairfax County Public Schools, Virginia

Introduction – *Second Edition*

Paula Patrick did an amazing job with this text when ACTFL first published it in 2007. As a helpful resource, it filled a gap as a concise "go to" guide for new language educators. As a district coordinator, I provided copies to all new language teachers and used it in professional development with them.

However, time has passed since this handbook was first published. Concepts of planning, instruction, and grading have evolved, proficiency-based Can-Do Statements have been created, and, of course, the available tools and resources have changed a great deal in twelve years. When this text was originally published, overhead projectors were common in classrooms, students rarely had their own cell phones, and social media were still relatively new. It seems that in the blink of an eye all of that has changed. The instructional environment is different, as are the tools and resources available to teachers.

Amid all of the ways in which teaching has changed in the past twelve years, much remains the same. Learners still need to be meaningfully engaged with the language. Educators must plan opportunities for learning that are relevant for learners. Students must believe that teachers care for them as individuals. Language and intercultural skills are increasingly important in our global society. Teaching is difficult, and educators new to the profession need support and guidance.

New teachers must learn a great deal, regardless of the amount of preparation they have before entering the classroom. The difficulty in working on this project is deciding how much information to provide to help new educators without overwhelming them. Much more depth on any concept could go into this guide. However, I have tried to find the appropriate balance, providing basic practical information, suggestions, and templates, without going into the detail found in a more comprehensive methods textbook. I hope this second edition of *The Keys to the Classroom* captures the wisdom Paula shared in the first edition, with changes and additions that meet the needs of new language educators in today's rapidly changing environment.

Leslie Baldwin, Ed.D.
World Languages Program Manager
Winston-Salem/Forsyth County Schools, North Carolina

Table of Contents

Foreword i

Dedication iii

Introduction – *First Edition*..v

Introduction – *Second Edition*..vii

Chapter 1: Why Language Education?
Why Did You Become a Language Educator? 1
Why Do Students Take Language Courses?.. 1
Language Proficiency.. 1
Performance vs. Proficiency... 2

Chapter 2: Where Do I Start?
Successful Planning and Goal-Setting... 5
Can-Do Statements... 5
Unit and Lesson Plans 6
Backward Design... 6
Assessments 8
Types of Assessments.. 9
Grading System 10
Standards-Based and Traditional Grading 10
Make-up Work... 11
First Week's Lessons.. 12
90%+ Target Language Use 12
Instructional Time: Use Every Minute 14
Equipment and Materials.. 15
Special Needs Students 17
Am I Ready?... 19

Templates:
Template A: Unit Plan Template... 20
Template B: Lesson Plan Template... 21
Template C: Simplified Lesson Plan Template... 22
Template D: Example Lesson Plan.. 23
Template E: Unit Design Reflection Checklist... 25
Template F: Lesson Design Reflection Checklist.. 26
Template G: Formative Assessment Task Template 1................................. 27
Template H: Example Formative Assessment Task..................................... 28
Template I: Example Integrated Performance Assessment (IPA) 29
Template J: Example Integrated Performance Assessment (IPA) 37
Successful Activity Checklist... 46

Chapter 3: How Do I Prepare?
Classroom Management... 47
Classroom Rules 47
Seating Arrangements 48
Student Names 49
Dress for Success 49
Creating a Language- and Culture-Rich Environment............................... 50
Organizing for Efficiency 51
Opportunities for Communication with Parents and Guardians............... 52
Back-to-School Night... 52

Communicating Beyond the Classroom. 55
Connections with Learners 56
Student Recognition. 56
Letters and Endorsements for Students 57
Colleagues: A Valuable Resource 57
Am I Ready? 59

Templates:
Template K: Classroom Rules 61
Template L: Student Responsibility 62
Template M: Class Participation. 63
Template N: Letter to Parents (Modern Language, Standards-Based Grading System). 64
Template O: Letter to Parents (Classical Language, Traditional Grading) 66
Template P: Information for Parents (Modern Language, Traditional Grading) 68
Template Q: Recommendation for Student 70
Template R: Thank You Letter 71
Template S: Invitation to School Event. 72

Chapter 4: How Do I Handle Challenging Moments?

The Traveling Teacher. 73
Mid-Lesson Changes 73
Emergency Lesson Plans. 74
Technology Malfunctions. 75
Interruptions 75
Student Confrontation 76
The Unexpected Parent Visit. 77
The Difficult Parent Conference 77
Difficult Responses 77
Medical Emergencies 78
Experiencing a Lockdown or National Emergency 79
Am I Ready for Challenging Moments? 81

Templates:
Template T: Emergency Lesson Plan 1 82
Template U: Emergency Lesson Plan 2. 83

Chapter 5: How Do I Grow?

Continuous Improvement 85
Revisions for Next Year 87
Successful Solutions 88
Teacher Evaluation and Observations 88
Professional Organizations 89
Professional Learning Network 90
Overseas Travel/Educational Trips. 90
Am I prepared for professional growth? 92

Appendices:
Appendix A: Oral Proficiency Levels in the Workplace. 93
Appendix B: World-Readiness Standards 94
Appendix C: NCSSFL-ACTFL Can-Do Statements 95
Appendix D: Guiding Principles and Core Practices for World Language Learning. 96
Appendix E: Reflection and Self-Assessment: The TELL Framework. 97

Afterword **98**

Acknowledgments **100**

Chapter 1 | Why Language Education?

Language educators choose this profession for a variety of reasons. Some are passionate about language and culture and want to share that passion with young people. Others want to help learners acquire language skills to ensure their access to a wide range of opportunities in today's world. Some educators feel that teaching is their calling, and language is the content with which they feel most comfortable. Whatever your motivation, welcome to this exciting and vital profession! This guide will help you enjoy a successful start and avoid potential pitfalls.

Why Did You Become a Language Educator?

Maybe you are a native speaker of the target language and want to share your heritage with others. Maybe you had a peer from another country who inspired you to learn another language, and now you want to teach it to others. Or maybe you had an influential language teacher in your own K–12 experience and you want to follow in that teacher's footsteps. Regardless of your reasons and the path that led you here, you now have your first job as a language teacher, and you need to get started. This book is designed to help you prepare for and succeed in your first year of teaching. Each chapter contains explanations of important concepts, reflection questions, and examples for you to use.

Why Do Students Take Language Courses?

Just as teachers have many reasons for becoming educators, so do students for wanting to learn a language. Some take language classes because it is a graduation or college entrance requirement. How will you engage their interest in the language? Others are taking your class because they think it will be interesting and truly want to learn a language. How will you build on that interest and push them to learn new skills? When surveyed, most students report that the main goal for taking language classes is to learn to communicate with other people. They do not say that their goal is to memorize vocabulary and conjugate verbs in as many tenses as possible. They want to be able to communicate and interact with people from other countries and cultures. While they may not know the terms to say it, what they seek is to achieve a proficiency level in the language to help them communicate with others: interpret meaning, exchange and negotiate meaning, and create meaning. How will you help learners meet this goal?

Language Proficiency

You have likely been asked whether you are "fluent" in a language other than your native tongue. But what does "fluent" mean? And how do you know whether you have attained "fluency"? In the field of language learning, "proficiency" is a more accurate term than "fluency." Language skills are measured by the *ACTFL Proficiency Guidelines*, which help to describe where learners are on a continuum of language skills and how well they can communicate. Your instructional goals should be geared toward developing proficiency, so it is important to understand proficiency and how this will affect your planning and instruction.

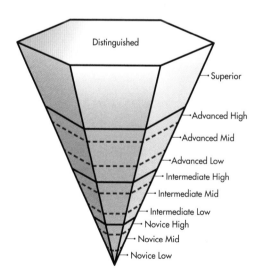

The ACTFL Proficiency Scale has five main levels as illustrated by the inverted pyramid: Novice, Intermediate, Advanced, Superior, and Distinguished. The first three levels are divided into sub-levels: low, mid, and high. The pyramid graphic is three-dimensional and inverted to help represent the progression of the proficiency levels.

Proficiency Levels and Descriptions

Proficiency Level	Summary Description
Novice	• Short, formulaic messages using memorized words/phrases • Highly familiar, predictable contexts
Intermediate	• Can recombine material for personal meaning • Sentences and strings of sentences • Mostly familiar contexts
Advanced	• Abundant language • Paragraph level • Familiar and unfamiliar contexts • Narrate with consistent use of multiple time frames
Superior	• Extended discourse • Abstract and hypothetical contexts
Distinguished	• Highly sophisticated, organized discourse • Wide range of highly abstract and hypothetical contexts • Cultural and historical references

A Novice Low learner, the lowest level on the scale, knows very little language and is extremely limited in communication skills. This puts the Novice Low learner at the one-word level, not yet able to use two-or-more-word phrases.

As the learner progresses through the sub-levels, the language increases both in amount and complexity. Not only does an Intermediate Low learner simply know more language than a Novice Mid learner does, more importantly, an Intermediate Low learner can do more with language and has more functional and independent use of language than a Novice Mid learner.

When examining the descriptions of each level of proficiency, the words "perfect" or "error-free" do not appear, as that is unrealistic even for native speakers. What develops across the proficiency continuum are a decrease in first-language interference and an increase in the ease with which someone can be understood.

What is your proficiency level in your second (or third or fourth) language? In most states, proof of a high level of proficiency is required for teacher licensure, so you have likely taken a language proficiency assessment. Appendix A shows the proficiency level needed to function in a language in various professions. To learn more about the Proficiency Guidelines, find detailed descriptions of each sub-level, and see examples in multiple languages at various proficiency levels, see the *ACTFL Proficiency Guidelines 2012* at www.actfl.org.

Performance vs. Proficiency

The differences between performance and proficiency must be clearly understood. You may notice an apparent discrepancy between what the *ACTFL Proficiency Guidelines* indicate about a learner's skills and what the proficiency level exit expectations are for a course in your state standards. For example, the sub-level description for Intermediate High includes a learner's ability to write in paragraphs at times, but your state standards say that your high school Level 2 students should be at the Novice High or Intermediate Low sub-level by the end of the course. You know that you will be able to guide these students to write in paragraphs, but that skill is not included in the sub-level description for Novice High or Intermediate Low. You just discovered the difference between performance and proficiency.

> ✓ *Repeated* performance leads to proficiency.

Proficiency is a measure of what a language learner can do independently, outside of the classroom, *without the support of your instruction*. When a learner must interact in the target language independently, without any of the scaffolded support in your classroom (a poster on the wall, a placemat of key vocabulary to use, an online translator for help, etc.), that is proficiency.

Performance is what learners do in the classroom with help and guidance from you. You will provide graphic organizers, sentence starters, question stems, examples, etc., to help your students learn and use the target language. These supports help

Performance	Proficiency
Based on classroom instruction (curriculum-dependent)	Independent of specific classroom instruction, curriculum, or when, where, or how the language was acquired
Language is developed in an instructional setting	Spontaneous, non-rehearsed interaction in real-world situations
Familiar contexts and content areas	Broad context/content in authentic situations
Learners acquire the functions, related structures, and vocabulary through a variety of tasks to get ready for the final performance assessment tasks related to a specific topic/theme.	Sustained performance (repeated and consistent) across all tasks and contexts for the level

learners to perform in the language, but within a controlled environment and with known topics.

Remember, *learners must practice performing like the next proficiency level up from theirs in order to eventually achieve that proficiency level*. Language learners have achieved the next proficiency level once they can use language in that way without the teacher's support. To follow the paragraph writing example, a learner will need much input and experience assembling sentences into an organized paragraph, with scaffolded support, before that learner can do it independently. But if learners are at the Intermediate Low sub-level and you, the teacher, assign only tasks that require isolated sentences but never ask them to write paragraphs, they cannot reach a higher proficiency level. The table above explains the basic differences.

Understanding this concept is important as you begin to think about unit and lesson planning. You need to know what the proficiency expectations are in order to plan instruction that helps learners achieve those levels. Aligning your tasks to the appropriate proficiency level will help them perform at that level, eventually leading to independence with those language skills. There will be more about this in Chapter 2!

Chapter 2 | Where Do I Start?

A new school year is about to begin. You're excited, and maybe a bit nervous. There is so much to do, and you have many questions to ask: *What do I do the first day and the first week? What exactly am I supposed to teach? How do I engage my learners and use resources effectively? How will I assess performance and assign grades?* It's time to think about all of these things and formulate some answers. This chapter will focus on planning assessment and instruction to help you get started. Templates and checklists at the end of the chapter will help you with the planning process.

Successful Planning and Goal-Setting

Standards-based education has grown since the 1990s and shaped the way teachers devise goals, develop lessons, and evaluate student performance. Standards-based education requires teachers to identify what learners will be able to do and what they should know by the end of the lesson or unit. Thus you must keep course goals and objectives firmly in focus as you develop lesson plans and assessments.

The course objectives will likely be determined by your state standards and district curriculum. If this is the case, please refer to your state and local curriculum guides when planning. Be sure your long-term and short-term goals align with your standards. Many state standards align with the *World-Readiness Standards for Learning Languages* and the ACTFL Proficiency Scale. The Standards include five goal areas, often referred to as "the 5 Cs":

- Communication (Interpretive, Interpersonal, Presentational)
- Cultures
- Connections
- Comparisons
- Communities

Communication is emphasized as the first goal area; the other four areas provide meaningful content to explore using the target language.

There are three types, or modes, of communication: Interpretive, Interpersonal, and Presentational. Interpretive communication involves listening, reading, and viewing. This is one-way communication in which learners receive input through what they hear, read, or view. Interpersonal communication occurs between two or more people. The interpersonal mode is two-way communication, involving an exchange of ideas or information, as in a conversation or discussion. Presentational communication is one-way, but is the opposite of the interpretive mode. Presentational communication involves speaking, writing, or use of media, but does not include interaction or an exchange with the intended audience. For example, a learner recording a video or creating a meme in the target language would use presentational communication.

The other "Cs," or goal areas, support the modes of communication. If learners are to communicate and use the target language in meaningful ways, they must do so with components of the other goals. **Cultures** include the products, practices, and perspectives of the target culture. **Connections** to other disciplines provide context for the language. Learners can make **Comparisons** of their own and the target language and culture. The **Communities** goal takes the language outside the walls of the classroom. (If you are not familiar with the *World-Readiness Standards for Language Learning*, see Appendix B.)

Typically local districts use the state standards to develop their specific curricula. Many districts have developed common thematic units for all languages so that, regardless of the target language, students learn about the same topics and themes.

> ❓ How are your state standards and district curriculum aligned to the "5 Cs"?

Can-Do Statements

Another component of planning and goal setting is the use of Can-Do Statements, which help connect the *ACTFL Proficiency Guidelines* and the *World-Readiness Standards* to student-friendly language so learners can set language learning goals and focus on progress toward those goals. Can-Do Statements can help learners understand the continua of proficiency levels and where they are on that scale.

Can-Do Statements can be used in conjunction with state standards by stating the local unit objectives in the first person for learners, and adapting the Can-Do Statements specifically to the context and content area of each unit. You can align Can-Do Statements to unit and lesson goals so students are aware of why they learn particular skills and then see how their performance on assessments provides proof that they "can do" a specific language function within a specific context and on a specific topic. (For more on Can-Do Statements, see Appendix C.)

When you develop course goals for a grading period, consider the themes and topics you will cover during that period of time. Use the same process to indicate what students should be able to do in each of the standards relative to the topics taught. Include Can-Do Statements that align to the goals. For example, teachers in Winston-Salem/Forsyth County, North Carolina, have included the following goals and Can-Do Statements for the Level 1 common thematic unit "Families and Communities, Topic: Connecting with Others." Formative and summative assessments in the unit plans have students show whether they can meet these goals in the applicable modes of communication. Learners will be able to:

- Describe self, friends, family and pets (physical characteristics, personality traits, preferences)
- Compare their lives to those of others (family, interests, daily routine)
- Express preferences (sports, activities)
- Exchange information with others about their preferences, relationships and connections to others
- Identify family characteristics around the world
- Make plans to do things with others

> ❓ Do you need to learn more about the three modes of communication and proficiency levels? See the *ACTFL Proficiency Guidelines 2012* and the *NCSSFL-ACTFL Can-Do Statements*, at www.actfl.org.

Can-Do Statements

Interpretive
- I can recognize familiar names and places in a video.
- I can understand what information is provided on an ID card.
- I can identify the preferred products and practices in my own and other cultures.

Presentational
- I can say my name, age, and where I live to introduce myself.
- I can write my personal information on a simple form.
- I can label items I like/dislike in a photo collage.

Interpersonal
- I can ask and answer questions to get to know someone—name, age, nationality, etc.
- I can ask and answer questions about my likes/dislikes/preferences.

When teachers write goals like these and use Can-Do Statements, then learners, parents, and administrators know what the concrete expected language outcomes are. Assessments and lesson plans must align with these goals. If your district does not provide a curriculum or unit plans, you may want to visit websites of other districts to see if course descriptions, syllabi, and goals are posted so you can have examples with which develop your own goals.

Unit and Lesson Plans

Planning for instruction is one of the most important keys to success in the classroom. Reflective educators consider the progress learners made in previous lessons and plan carefully for the next steps, remembering to distinguish between an agenda or itinerary (i.e., a list of activities that you plan to do) and a unit or lesson plan that identifies key student learning outcomes.

Backward Design

The most important component of planning for learning is the concept of backward design. You must know your goals before figuring out how to accomplish them. Common analogies for this process include the need for a map to arrive at a

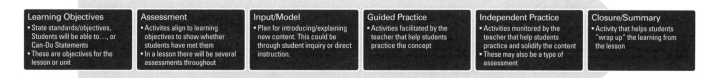

Backward Design Process for Units and Lessons

particular destination, or the need for blueprints to construct a building. Before you start to drive on a road trip, you must know your destination to figure out how to get there, and to know whether you've arrived there.

> ❓ If you don't know your end goal, then how do you know when or whether you achieved the goal?

The same is true of lesson and unit planning. You must start with the end in mind. First, identify the standards or learning objectives (and possibly related Can-Do Statements) that will be assessed at the end of the lesson or unit. Then develop the assessment that will let you know whether learners have met the objective. Once you have determined how you will assess whether learners meet the objective, then you can plan for the instructional activities that will guide them to success on the assessment. Too often new teachers fall into the trap of planning today for tomorrow, then getting close to where they think a unit should be ending, and deciding what the assessment will look like. This process is stressful and overwhelming! You will be much better prepared, and more able to plan effective lessons, if you (and the learners) know what they should be able to do and how they will show it at the end of the unit. Notice that the emphasis in planning is on what learners can do, reflecting growth along the proficiency continuum, not on what the teacher is teaching. The unit plan identifies the goal in terms of what learners can do; then, each daily lesson identifies steps to develop the knowledge and skills necessary for learners to achieve that goal. Assessment at the end of a unit, therefore, does not focus on what learners simply know, such as vocabulary or grammatical structures. End-of-unit assessments need to focus on what learners can do with what they know.

In a backward design process, always work from the biggest idea back to the smallest. This means, if a common school or district assessment will occur at the end of the course, you need to understand what students must do on that summative assessment and then plan units from there. Unit assessments should help prepare students for the course assessment. After

planning a unit, if district unit plans are not already provided, only then should you begin to plan for daily lessons. Use the learning objectives for the unit to work backward and guide daily instruction, constantly knowing what students will be required to do at the end of the unit, so that each day builds toward that language performance. Example unit and lesson plan templates are included in this chapter to help you think through the necessary components.

> ❓ Does your school or district require a specific lesson plan template? Ask your mentor or a colleague to be sure.

At the end of the unit and lesson-planning process, teachers should be able to answer the following questions:

- How is this plan aligned with the state and national world language standards?
- How does your plan encourage your students to take responsibility for their own learning?
- How will your students use their knowledge to function in authentic, real-life situations?
- How do your tasks provide ways for your students to demonstrate their learning?
- How will you evaluate the effectiveness of your plan?

In developing a lesson plan, be sure to:

- Identify the language and level for the lesson.
- Note the theme and topic for the lesson.
- List the resources that will be used to implement the lesson.
- Identify the standards and proficiency level target the lesson will address. For example, Novice High Presentational Communication.
- Indicate the learning objectives. These should align to state standards and could be phrased as an "I can" statement to be student-friendly. For example, a Novice High presentational objective from the North Carolina state standards is: "Create simple phrases and short sentences in spoken or written presentations to provide

information about familiar topics." A related Can-Do Statement would be: "I can write phrases and simple sentences to describe the activities I like to do."

- Explain how the teacher will assess the learners' performance and/or acquired knowledge throughout the lesson.
- Explain the design of the activities. Describe what learners will do and how the learning will take place, such as paired activities or small groups.
- As you plan activities, consider what you will do as the teacher, and what students will be doing as the learners. For example, if you are showing a video or playing an audio selection, students should have an active role, such as filling out a graphic organizer as they watch or listen.
- Consider the primacy/recency effect, which means that we remember first and last learned subjects best, but not middle ones. Therefore, as teachers, we should create many "firsts" and "lasts" in lessons by chunking the time. Be sure to include multiple activities; none should take more than 15 minutes to complete.
- Include more than one mode of communication. For example, students should not spend 45 minutes doing all Interpretive Reading/Listening. Plan the flow so that an interpretive reading activity (input) leads to an interpersonal activity (supported output), which then leads to a presentational speaking or writing activity (more independent output).
- Plan for transitions between activities! For example, plan specifically for how you will collect an assignment and then begin a new task, or how you will regain the students' attention when it is time for a partner activity to end before moving on to the next task.
- Especially in modern languages, plan to stay in the target language 90%+ of class time. This 90%+ target language slogan reminds all language educators to provide an environment of immersion in the target language, so that almost everything learners hear, read, view, say, write, or experience is in that language. This requires thinking about how you will introduce activities and give instructions, provide explanations, and present the language so students can comprehend it without English translation. As a new teacher, you may want to script what you will say until this becomes a more natural process for you.

- Prepare examples/models ahead of time. Don't wait until you're in the middle of instruction to think of your examples.
- Plan for providing feedback on assessments so students can learn to improve. For performance assessments, a rubric will help you to give feedback efficiently and consistently. For some assignments, peer editing can be used.
- Ask students to reflect on what they have learned, as a full class or in small groups. A closing or summarizing activity helps students to manage their own learning. Some teachers require students to keep journals and, at the end of the period, to write their thoughts or a brief summary of what they have learned. Also, ask students to give examples of what they have learned to demonstrate their mastery of the lesson material.
- If you think through all aspects of lesson instruction and desired learner outcomes before entering the classroom, you will more successfully convey to your students why they are doing what you ask of them, and how it fits in the larger picture of their learning experience. And you will more effectively assess their performance and pinpoint sections of the lesson you may need to re-address. A well-developed lesson also reduces the probability that you will teach a grammatical structure simply because it comes next in the chapter, or assign students to do a textbook exercise simply because it falls under the just-introduced grammar concept.

After each lesson planning process, note in your plan book what worked well and what might need improvement. This will save you time in future lessons. (Example unit and lesson plan templates, as well as planning checklists, are at the end of the chapter.)

Assessments

Assessing student achievement in a standards-based classroom means learners will be assessed more frequently on what they *can do* in the language rather than what they merely know about it. This means that open-ended performance tasks will be administered periodically so that learners can be assessed on their progress.

We have long known that students study or pay attention to that which they think will be formally assessed. A common question you'll get from students when you introduce a topic is, "Will we be tested on this?" In other words, "Do we really have to know this?" But teachers often play the same game when they announce, "Listen carefully to what I am teaching you today, because you will be tested on this on Friday." What both the teacher and the student are doing is categorizing portions of a lesson as "important" and "not important."

Since assessments should always mirror instruction, teachers should assess for student performance rather than isolated vocabulary words or discrete verb forms. If the goal of teaching a language is to have students communicate in it, teachers should evaluate their students to see if they can indeed use the vocabulary and structures in context to communicate thoughts and ideas.

Many educators have embraced the standards-based instructional model, and teachers are asked to write standards-based lesson plans, but time and again teachers fall back on the selected-response test format with the opinion that it is faster to grade and "more accurate" in terms of a definite answer without arguments. But if you are going to look at the big picture when you plan a lesson, ask yourself, "What is it I want my learners to be able to do at the end of this lesson?" Then use your district's measurement tool or design a measurement tool that indicates all of what the students can do at the end of the lesson, not merely what they have memorized and were able to recognize briefly during the test. Performance assessments can take longer to grade, but when you become comfortable using a rubric, the pace of grading each assessment picks up.

Note that teachers should use a variety of assessments and a balance in terms of types of assessments. This means that not every type of assessment must be used in every unit. Make sure that any summative (end-of-unit) assessments reflect the unit's learning goals and that any formative (mid-point checks) assessments reflect preparation for and progress toward that final summative assessment.

Types of Assessments

You have already seen the terms "formative" and "summative" relating to assessment in this text, and you will likely hear them often in your school. It is important to understand the difference between formative and summative assessments.

Formative assessment is assessment *for* learning. These are tasks all along the way that help learners improve and give you, the teacher, feedback on how students are progressing toward an objective. As learners receive feedback from you on formative assessments, they find out what they are doing well and how they can improve on a particular learning goal. You might find that students aren't progressing with a concept as quickly as you thought, so you need to adjust your daily lesson plans accordingly.

Formative assessments might be an impromptu writing assignment in class, a short learning check, or a quick summary activity at the end of a lesson. Quick formative assessments should occur throughout a lesson, enabling students to practice and giving you information on their progress toward the learning objectives. You will want to collect data for some formative assessments. For others you will simply take mental notes to guide the lesson's progress.

For example, you might use a rubric to assign points and provide feedback to students on a draft-writing task, which would also give you data on students' progress. Many online tools that let students practice automatically collect data on their performance that can help you assess their progress. For a task such as an individual white board activity in which students write or draw responses to an oral prompt, when they hold up their boards you can quickly scan the room to see how they are responding and determine their readiness to move to the next task.

All of these formative assessments provide some kind of feedback for students so that they can work toward the learning objectives. They also provide various kinds of data to inform your planning and instruction.

Summative assessment, by contrast, is assessment *of* learning. It happens at the end of a unit, semester, or year. This might be a culminating project, a unit assessment, or a final exam. Formative assessments should be designed to prepare students for the summative assessment. The summative assessment should not be a "gotcha" experience for students, containing unknown content or trying to trick them with something unexpected. Since you have planned your summative assessment at the beginning of the unit, you and the learners should be aware of what the expectations are (that is, how good is good enough) and what they will be asked to do.

Formative Assessment	Summative Assessment
For learning	*Of* learning
Throughout lessons and units	End of unit/semester/year
Learners receive timely feedback	Learners receive timely feedback (but typically can't use feedback to improve on that assessment)
Teacher uses student performance data to inform daily instruction/planning	Teacher uses student performance data to inform long-range planning

Your lessons and formative assessments throughout the unit should lead students to success on the summative assessment. You may have heard that teaching to the test is a bad thing, but in helping learners to prepare for and succeed on a summative task, you are actually teaching to the test in a good way! (Examples of summative assessments and rubrics are at the end of this chapter.)

To develop an assessment system that truly monitors learners' progress in developing communicative competence, consider these strategies for managing performance assessment:

- *Give a performance assessment in lieu of a chapter test.* If the learners understand the rubric and what you expect them to be able to do, they should be able to show you what they have learned in a more meaningful way than filling in blanks on a form.
- *Divide assessments by levels or class periods.* For example, odd period classes can occur one week, even period classes the next week. If you assess all students on one day, the grading process will be overwhelming and it will take you longer to present the results to your students. Feedback to learners is what makes a rubric much better than simply a grade as an indicator of progress and areas that need improvement. If your students don't get feedback from you in a timely fashion, they'll have more difficulty knowing where they need to improve before the next assessment.
- *Plan for multiple formative assessments throughout the unit.* This will help prepare learners for the summative assessment.
- *Don't try to correct every mistake.* Simply highlight only the errors that pertain to the assignment's goals. Some students do not digest all comments teachers write on the papers. If learners are taught how to analyze their mistakes and make revisions on their own or with a peer, this will increase their capacity to self-correct.
- *Replace traditional quizzes with formative tasks.* As long as the task is well-written (with clear objectives, minimum requirements, and a scenario to set the scene)

students should be able to show you how much they have learned.

Grading System

One of the hardest changes students face when transitioning from elementary school to middle and high school is having a different teacher and classroom for each subject. In each teacher's class, they may face a new set of rules, a different grading system, and different classroom procedures. Your school or district may have grading policies and procedures you need to note. To help your students, post your grading policy for all to see at any time. Also, include your grading policy in the information for parents and guardians and in your syllabus. Students and parents and guardians alike will appreciate the opportunity to refer to this information during the year to review your system.

Standards-Based and Traditional Grading

Educators use two basic student performance evaluation systems. Your school or department may require a particular one.

A **traditional grading system**, the most common, has various categories of grades, each with a different weight. For example, tests, quizzes, and classwork, with tests constituting higher percentages of the grade than classwork. You are likely familiar with such a system from your own experience as a student. Likewise, your students and parents and guardians will be most familiar and comfortable with this type of grading system.

The advantages of a traditional system are that it is relatively easy to manage the logistics, and it is clear to students and parents. A disadvantage is that it can be hard for students to bring their grade back up after just a few very low grades in heavier weighted categories. Counting every assignment actually penalizes learners, as their "practice" (where they experiment and take risks to try to use language in new ways) counts against them when included with the scores showing any improvement in subsequent tasks or assessments. Additionally, grades may not be an accurate reflection of a student's growth or current knowledge and skills.

A **standards-based system**, however, requires teachers to align assignments to a curriculum's standards or objectives. There may still be various categories of different weights, but the categories, rather than assignment types, can be aligned to the standards. For example, your categories could include Interpretive Communication, Interpersonal Communication, and Presentational Communication, rather than tests, classwork, and homework. Additionally, standards-based grading is often aligned with the use of mastery learning. This practice allows learners to submit and re-submit evidence of learning that aligns with a particular standard until they reach an acceptable level of mastery. If you are not familiar with this concept, use of mastery learning will require your own research and learning.

> ✓ To be equitable, grades should reflect what learners know and can do, not behavior or participation in activities not related to content.

The following points will help you to be consistent and clear about how you intend to grade your learners' progress:

- *Consider what you truly value as evidence of learners' demonstrating success, as evidence of their achievement of your learning goals.* Then ensure that your grading system reflects what you value and rewards learners for reaching those goals.
- *Decide from the beginning whether you will be using points or percentages.* Switching between the two systems is very confusing.
- *Determine categories for grades.* Consider whether you will use a standards-based system or a more traditional grading system. Consider whether your grades will be based on the three modes of communication, or other categories.
- *Make sure learners understand how each grading period will be calculated, along with the final exam, to come up with the final grade for the year.* Again, there may be district or school policies regarding exam weights of which you need to be aware.
- *Decide whether you will allow students to submit late assignments or retake assessments.* These are important components of mastery learning.

- *Decide whether you will offer extra credit opportunities.* This is not needed in a standards-based grading system, since missing assignments are not held against the learner who eventually demonstrates achievement of the learning target, goal or expectation.
- *Explain to students how much weight each category will have.*
- *Give students a quick example of all of the grades that could go into a grading period.* Ask them to make the computations. This exercise will impress upon them the weight of different categories, and you will see students putting forth more effort in the areas with more weight.
- *When you use a rubric for performance assessments or projects, give students a copy of it before the assessment or assignment is given.* Learners should be informed about the criteria for grading before, not after, the project is completed. Remember: learners will give you what you ask for. If you did not make your criteria for grading clear, you will not receive a quality project in return. Learners perform best when given clear expectations and directions, not left to guess what the teacher expects.

Post the school district's policy for what constitutes an A, B, C, D, and F. It may seem clear to you, but some students may have transferred to your school from another district, and they may be unfamiliar with elements of your district's grading policy, such as the cut-off percentages for achieving A, B, C, or D.

> ❓ Does your school or district have common rubrics that you are expected to use for assessments in each mode of communication? Ask your mentor or a colleague.

Make-up Work

When teachers have more than 100 students in their charge, just staying on top of make-up work can be an arduous task. You should have a policy for making up homework assignments, quizzes, projects, and tests. Make your policy clear to students and parents and guardians during the first week of school, and reinforce it during the first grading period. Your policy should include:

- How a student can obtain the assignment if absent.

- When a student can come after school to take a make-up assessment.
- A deadline for make-up work, and details about how many class sessions the student is allowed to make up after each absence. (Note: If a school is on A/B day scheduling, it can be confusing to state how many "days" a student has, because the class meets every other day.)
- A deadline for extended absences. If a student has been out for a week or longer, you should communicate a plan to enable the student to submit the work, keeping in mind that the student also has five or six other classes of make-up work.
- Your expectations of the student, and the consequences if a project deadline is missed due to an absence.
- The consequences for not making up work.

When assigning make-up work for an extended absence, keep in mind that some assignments could be shortened or eliminated. For example, if the student can learn a particular language structure after one 10-sentence exercise, perhaps the other four similar exercises can be omitted. For a two- or three-week absence, look at the long-range objectives and reconsider and revise the daily homework exercises. The student needs to feel able to keep up with this class along with other classes. Perhaps a tutor can be recommended, or after-school sessions can be set up when the student returns to make sure certain elements have been learned.

First Week's Lessons

The first week is always interesting. Teachers who develop lessons for the full class period sometimes run out of time. Know what all of your responsibilities will be during your first week before writing lesson plans for that week. In the first few days of school, many schools require teachers to distribute and collect important documents and go over fire-drill information, student responsibilities and rights, supplies needed, course information, and classroom rules. These are important to address, but consider starting the class by engaging learners with language before getting into the logistics. Plan engaging activities, using the target language from the beginning, to "hook" the students. Then address the necessary logistics after students have participated in learning activities. In high schools especially, students' schedules are often adjusted during the first two weeks of school, so be prepared for your class

rosters to change a bit in that time. This is a good time for use of the target language, getting to know your students, and helping them get to know one another. Here are suggested topics and activities for the first week:

Novice Low/Mid Levels

- Greetings and introductions
- Setting the tone for 90%+ target language use
- Cognates, if applicable
- Watching a video of a school from the target culture to make predictions and comparisons
- Overview of Proficiency Levels

Novice High Level

- Student introductions
- Student discussions on family, leisure time activities, likes and dislikes
- "All About Me" posters: Each student makes a poster describing his/her key physical and social characteristics
- Review of themes and topics from level 1, integrated into activities as a review, while teaching new material

Intermediate Low/Mid Levels

- Detailed student introductions
- Discussion of students' summer activities or travel
- Discussion of current events
- Movie and/or book critiques
- Describing pictures (to encourage students to use adjectives and detailed descriptions in the target language)

Intermediate Mid/High Levels

- Activities involving assigned summer reading
- Discussion of current events
- Movie and/or book critiques
- Discussion and reflection regarding student responsibilities and suggestions for changes in school policies
- Comparison of environmental policies between the U.S. and the target language country

90%+ Target Language Use

You have already seen references to the need for "90%+ target language use," one of the Core Practices, found in Appendix D. An extremely important concept to understand and apply,

"90%+ target language use" means you provide an immersive environment in the classroom, maximizing target language use, and you teach *in*, rather than *about*, the language. For modern languages with active Interpersonal Communication within the cultures that speak the language, such as Chinese, Arabic, Spanish, or French, maximized immersion in and use of target language by teachers and students is a must. There is debate about whether this applies to classical languages, such as Latin and Ancient Greek. If you teach a classical language, discuss this with your mentor or colleagues. The *Standards for Classical Language Learning* emphasize that, while reading is the primary goal, some Interpersonal conversation is helpful to build fluency.

Constant use of the target language helps to establish an immersive environment and shows learners that the language is not a list of things to memorize, but a vehicle for natural communication. This is true at all levels of language, including and especially at the Novice level. If a world-language class is conducted mostly in English, with the target language used only for specific activities, then students are learning *about* the language, instead of learning to *communicate* in the language. The goal of a language class is for learners to build proficiency skills and use the language for meaningful purposes, which is not attainable if the teacher and students use English most the time.

Staying in the target language for instruction requires thoughtful planning. You must use comprehensible input so students will understand and learn. This involves using gestures, visuals, and objects to show meaning. Repetition, modeling, use of cognates, and a slower-than-native rate of speech are key components of comprehensible input. You will need to prepare models and examples to help students understand the expectations for a task or activity.

Giving instructions and dealing with minor management issues are an important part of maximizing target language use. For example, if you are asking Novice level students to get out a sheet of paper and a pen or pencil, do so in the target language, not English, while holding up a piece of paper and a pencil to illustrate your meaning. Students will understand and get the gist of your meaning. They need not understand every word you say, nor identify the verb form being used. They just need to understand enough to get out the materials you have requested. If you need to tell a student to move to another seat to help curb his/her inclination to talk to a neighbor, you can do so in the target language while pointing to another seat and motioning to pick up his/her materials and move.

Some teachers feel the need to say something in the target language and then repeat it in English, underestimating the ability of the students to understand. Do not fall into this temptation! As soon as students understand that you will do this, they will not listen to the target language and will wait for you to say it in English. This does not help them build proficiency in the target language. Helping learners to adjust to an immersive target language environment, especially at lower levels, is related to your classroom management. Students will ask you to say things in English, will say they don't understand, and will prod you to translate. Just as you have to be consistent with other components of management, the same is true for using the target language. Help them to learn that if they watch your modeling, gestures, and visuals they will understand what is needed.

> ✅ Creating an immersive target language environment is connected to your management plan. Be consistent and follow through with stated expectations for use of the target language—yours and theirs!

Teacher discourse is important in creating and perpetuating the target language environment. If the target language is not your native tongue, it may not be your habit to constantly use it in your own mind. When you talk out loud to yourself because you can't find the white board marker (yes, you will do this!), you must do so in the target language. When someone calls your classroom because a student needs to check out, answer the phone in the target language and respond to the caller's questions in it—"yes" and "no" in many languages are typically understood universally. The more consistent you are with using the target language and not English, the more it becomes habitual and natural for you, and students learn to expect it. You will find that students will start to pick up on common phrases, exclamations, and commands you use and begin to use them own their own.

Remember, 90%+ target language use is not just about you as the teacher, but also a rule for students. Even (and especially) at the Novice level, learners must be encouraged to use the language they know in order to communicate a message. That is why your language-rich environment (addressed in the next chapter) is important. When students say things in English that you know they can figure out in the target language, help them to do so by giving them examples to repeat, pointing to a resource on the wall, or motioning toward something on the board/screen that can help them. Eliciting student target language use is essential to helping them build communicative competency. (At the end of this chapter is a checklist to help you reflect upon whether meaningful target language use is the focus of your tasks and activities.)

Note that the Core Practice states 90%+, not 100%, in the target language. Any use of English should be specifically planned and targeted. In your lesson plans, decide when/where/if you might need to use English to explain a particular concept or clarify learners' understanding. The use of English (native language vs. target language) may be in a "private" sharing of learners' thinking with their teacher, such as to explain a deep understanding or inference learners gained in an interpretive task, but the explanation is not within the learners' control of target language. This might also be a time for student reflection on the Can-Do Statements. Have some kind of symbol or signal that indicates when you and they can use English. This should be an intentionally planned part of the lesson or unit, though it may not be needed each day.

Instructional Time: Use Every Minute

It takes a while to get the timing down for a class, be it 50 or 90 minutes long. The key to using every minute productively is to have a couple of extra activities planned in case of empty minutes at lesson's end. Time is not effectively used by simply telling students to use the extra 10 minutes at the end to finish homework, for this often signals to students that class is over, so they may feel free to chat, relax, and look at their phones and emails. Students are tired by now, and this 10-minute "start your homework" strategy ends up being counterproductive. Very few students want to dive in and get as much done as humanly possible within that short time frame; by the time they get all of their materials out to start their homework, they haven't enough time to complete it, so why start? Talking is more fun. Additionally, such an unstructured time can be a recipe for management issues in the classroom.

Students' learning must therefore have some type of closure activity, which could include:

- Divide the class into groups, and see which group is first to come up with "The five things we learned today."

- At the end of each lesson, require students to write in a journal a reflection of what they learned that day.
- Toss a soft ball around the class, allowing each student who catches it to ask another student what he learned in today's lesson.
- Have blank comic strips handy, and ask students to fill in the blank bubbles with a conversation pertinent to what they learned in class.
- Have students pick scenario cards and come in front of the class to act out a scene.
- Ask students to complete a "Ticket out the Door" (TOD) or "exit ticket." This could involve an essential question for them to answer, a quick review that helps them to summarize what was learned in the class, or some other type of lesson closure. TODs can be completed on Post-It notes or index cards, or through online tools such as a Google form or Padlet.com.
- Require students to make their own sets of vocabulary flashcards for each unit. Cards should have a picture on one side and the target language word written on the other. These can be used for "filler" activities at any time. Students can work individually or in pairs to study with the cards. For example, have pairs of students spread out a set of cards with the picture side up, call out the vocabulary word, and see who can pick up the correct flash card first. Or do the opposite: when students have the word side of the cards visible, show a visual or object and ask them to find the word first. Also, beyond mere vocabulary practice, ask students to determine how many phrases or sentences they can make by combining words (and sometimes adding in additional words with blank note cards provided).
- Individual white boards can be helpful tools in the language classroom. You can do many different activities with them, and they can be great for last-minute time filling activities. Students can draw what you say or describe. You say a basic math problem, and students write it on the boards; you show visuals or perform an action, and students write the word/sentence, etc. Students hold up their boards as they finish their response, and you can quickly gauge who knows it, who doesn't, or how much help might be needed with a particular topic. You can purchase white boards already made, or make your own. Shower board can be purchased and cut at a home improvement store. Heavy-duty plastic plates can also serve this purpose.

Activities such as these have no grades attached and are a good way to provide closure to the lesson, leaving students feeling that they have learned something and/or have performed spontaneously without the pressure of making a mistake. These are great closing activities to build self-esteem and keep the momentum going until time is up. Additionally, a closure activity is key for students' learning. The brain needs a summarizing activity to help solidify the learning.

Brain Breaks

Whether you have 45-minute or 90-minute classes, remember that learners must be able to move and have their brains activated in different ways. It is not reasonable to expect young people of any age to sit in their seats during an entire class, all day, every day. As a part of your planning, allow opportunities for movement and activating various parts of the brain to maximize learning. "Brain breaks" can be a good way to transition between other activities, integrate language and physical movement, and stimulate other areas of the brain. Activities that require crossing the body's midline in some way are particularly effective for activating both sides of the brain. Here are a few suggestions:

- *Clap and Spell:* Prepare envelopes or sealable plastic bags with sets of vocabulary words familiar to learners. Have students work in pairs. Give each pair a set of words. Students draw a word from the envelope or bag and spell it together in the target language, clapping opposite hands with one another for each letter. As a variation, instead of only providing the words, have the students draw from sets of flashcards with pictures on the fronts and corresponding vocabulary words on the backs. To spell the words they need to know what the pictures are, but if they aren't sure, they can check the backs of the cards.
- *Quick Math:* Working in pairs, students count to three in the target language simultaneously. After saying "three," each student shows a number of fingers on one hand. The student in the pair who says the sum of what s/he and his/her partner are showing the fastest wins a point. *Variation:* Have students multiply, subtract, or divide, rather than add the two numbers. For some languages this can also be a way for the students to naturally integrate culture, as showing numbers with fingers is done differently in different cultures.

- *Part-to-Part:* Working in pairs, students call out two body parts in the target language and touch those two parts together. For example, elbow-to-elbow, hand-to-knee, head-to-shoulder, etc. With this activity you must be careful about which body parts you say, and how the age group of your students will react to it. *Variation:* Have students work individually rather than in pairs. To make it more challenging, add instructions for left or right parts of the body.
- *Pick it Up:* This is similar to "Part-to-Part," but with an added challenge. Give each pair of students an item such as a spongy ball, or have students ball up pieces of paper to use. Rather than touching two body parts together, students use them to pick up the object.

Equipment and Materials

Before the first day of school, check the equipment that is in your classroom(s). Be sure you know what is available and how it works. This might include ensuring that the LCD projector has a working bulb, or that you know how to operate an interactive panel. Connect your laptop to a TV screen or play audio/video files so that all can hear and see. Also, be sure you have other needed materials: white board markers, erasers, etc.

It is frustrating to start a lesson, only to discover you aren't connected to the Internet or your laptop isn't communicating with the projector or flat panel. Stopping to troubleshoot such issues takes away precious class time and easily encourages your learners to be off task. Know who you need to contact (when and where) for instruction on unfamiliar tools, as well as repairs, and supplies. Have a backup plan in case a technology tool or device is not working.

Technology

Technology can be your friend or, at times, your worst enemy. Well ahead of opening day, ask your school what digital tools and resources are available for recording grades, contacting parents and guardians, accessing student information, posting homework on websites, creating lessons and delivering lessons, enhancing instruction, assessing student performance, etc. Once school starts, it is hard to find time to learn about and practice with the resources and devices available at your school.

> **?** How can you use components of blended learning to make your instruction more effective? You may want to discuss this with a mentor or other colleagues.

Find out early if your school's teachers can access a learning management system (LMS) and whether they are expected to use the LMS to deliver the course in a blended model. Ask if there is a particular platform and format for teachers' websites where you can post homework assignments and other information.

Helpful websites offer teachers tips and teaching freebies such as clip art, puzzles and games. Teacher websites contain a wealth of information. Always evaluate resources to ensure their alignment with your curriculum and objectives. Also bookmark websites of other local, regional, and national professional organizations that can assist you in your career. The benefits of becoming a member of professional organizations will be discussed later in this handbook.

Devices and Digital Resources

Many schools either set a "bring your own device" policy or provide laptops or tablets for student use on a "one-to-one" basis. It is easy to be charmed by the digital devices and resources now at the disposal of educators and learners alike. However, as an educator, it is your responsibility to evaluate your options and select the resources most appropriate for the learning goal or assessment. Countless online resources can aid instruction and assessment.

Instructional tools can take many forms. Pencil and paper are instructional tools, just as a laptop can be a tool. Choose the appropriate tool for the task. Some teachers fall into the trap of including a digital device or tool because it looks good and they've been told to incorporate technology. A wise instructional technology leader once gave the following analogy: No teacher ever looked at a pencil and said, "Wow! Look at this great pencil! I'm going to include using pencils in my lesson plan today, because this pencil is so flashy and cool!"

Just as you don't plan your lesson around the use of a pencil, you don't plan it around a cool new website or tablets the school just purchased. Determine your instructional goals first, and then identify the tools that will help learners to meet those goals in efficient and engaging ways. Sometimes using pencil and paper is the best way to achieve the goal, and sometimes the website that allows learners to create with language in different ways is the better choice.

> **✓** When considering how to effectively integrate technology and instruction, remember that it is about the task, not the tool.

Blended Learning

You may have heard of blended learning environments or experienced them as a learner. The use of blended learning depends upon the resources your school provides, as well as learners' ability to work online outside of school. Some schools/districts require elements of blended learning, either as a part of regular instruction or for unexpected cancelled days such as snow days. In such cases, all learners can access the Internet and appropriate devices outside of school, or those without such access are accommodated in other ways.

Blended learning is more than simply making information and assignments available online through an LMS or website. The actual learning occurs both in a traditional face-to-face classroom *and* in an online format. Students learn content and acquire skills outside of the traditional classroom through a variety of online tools and then extend the learning within the classroom.

Blended learning can occur in many different ways. A concept could be introduced by having students watch a video outside of class and complete an assignment related to that video, so that when they come to class the basic information has already been introduced and you can use class time to apply the concept or content. Also, students can access some content on their terms and at their own pace. For example, they can play the video as many times as needed, pause it, go back, etc.

True blended learning may not be feasible in your teaching context, depending upon the resources available to you and your students. If it is possible or required at your school, you will want to research this topic further, so you should request some professional development and support to use this concept effectively.

Help or Hindrance?

The use of cell phones in the classroom is often a source of debate. Some schools and educators have a "no phone" policy, while others embrace them as learning tools. Classroom management issues related to students' phones can frustrate teachers, so they decide to ban their use. Others have successfully managed the use of phones and other devices so they contribute to the learning process rather than detract from it.

As the teacher, you must establish routines and procedures enabling learners to use tools effectively without getting off task. Going back to the pencil vs. digital tool analogy above, schools most likely have not banned pencils and paper because passing notes in class distracted students. Nor should cell phones be restricted from classroom use. Consider how often you use your smartphone to learn or complete a professional task. Students are no different and must be taught responsible use of their devices, including how to use them as learning tools, not just for social media.

If available to students, cell phones can be helpful tools in many ways. Some educators let learners use their phones to record audio and video for interpersonal or presentational speaking assessments. Various apps can be used for this, or students can use the built-in camera and recorder on the phone and upload the files to a shared folder. Others can scan QR codes to lead to activities or take pictures for a scavenger hunt with clues provided in the target language. You might want to let learners use phones for the occasional need to look up a word while working on a task, though of course not for full translation of text. Learners might access your website or LMS for activities and assignments using their phones. Countless apps and sites can be useful in a language class; with constant changes in what is available, it is difficult to name examples.

Just as you will develop routines for procedures such as what students are expected to do when they enter the classroom or how they access assignments when they miss class, develop and teach routines for cell phone use. Below are ideas educators have found to be effective:

- Use a pocket chart where students are expected to put their phones upon entering class. When the time is appropriate, students can retrieve their phones for a learning purpose and return them to the pockets when finished. Number the pockets to assign students to particular spaces.

- Have a visual symbol, such as a reversible sign, that indicates when it's ok to have phones in use and when it is not permitted. This makes expectations clear to students.

Special Needs Students

This section is designed to help you create classroom environments that will meet all learners' needs in world language instruction. Specific strategies will augment the learning of those needing additional help. Seek professional development from your district's Exceptional Children (EC) office or meet with a resource teacher at your school to learn about the variety of strategies for helping students with Individualized Education Plans (IEPs) succeed in the classroom.

The Individuals with Disabilities Education Act Amendments (IDEA, 1977) encourage the inclusion of children with disabilities in the least restrictive environment (LRE) to the maximum extent appropriate with children who are not disabled. These laws and regulations change, so plan early on to visit the numerous websites where current information regarding EC can be found. All educators, including language teachers, may access support from EC staff members at their schools. An EC teacher should contact the language teacher early in the year regarding the students with disabilities in your classes. However, if EC staff do not contact you, pursue contact on your own initiative. You need to become aware of required accommodations early in the school year, preferably early enough to implement any accommodations needed before Back-to-School Night.

Language educators should express special education-related concerns and questions to the case manager or EC department. Language teachers may be asked to participate in IEP meetings. This process varies from school to school, in both frequency and format. You are advised to keep documentation and copies of all information you receive on this subject. You may participate in the IEP process of any of your students, whether or not this participation has been formally requested. In addition, you or a parent may request an IEP meeting at any time to address possible changes to accommodations and services.

Accommodations are legally binding. All teachers must implement, document, and adapt classroom materials and/or environment as identified within the IEP and the 504 plan, including making accommodations for assessments. If necessary, seek assistance to implement accommodations as written, and stay in contact with staff members, parents and guardians, and students regarding progress on these accommodations. You must keep documentation (i.e., work samples) that demonstrates each student's progress and use of accommodations. Parents have the right to request such documentation at any time.

Basic classroom strategies for accommodations:

- Allow students to choose seating options that help them learn, reserving the right to overrule their choices if they prove distracting.
- Allow choice of product for assignments. For example, give the option of a PowerPoint presentation, an electronic poster, or a hard copy to be submitted for a particular task.
- Allow students to have "fidgets," or items such as stress balls they can quietly manipulate during class to help maintain focus.
- Create a classroom climate in which students feel comfortable and involved.
- We often teach based on our own learning styles, so take multiple learning styles into account when planning instruction. Consider the needs of introverts and extroverts, those who learn musically and those who may not, those who benefit more from visual supports, etc.
- Help students develop the art of inference by making them aware of clues for intelligent guessing.
- Personalize instruction to motivate students to express themselves readily.
- Ask students to monitor each other's speech, thus taking an active role in teaching as well as learning.
- Present all material in a meaningful context and manner.
- Ask successful language learners to serve as informants regarding strategies, techniques, and study skills.
- Encourage learners with specific needs to experiment until they find their own particular learning styles.

Classroom participation:

- To encourage spontaneous oral communication, avoid overcorrection, which tends to inhibit learners' attempts to speak the language.
- Include age-appropriate situations and questions in daily speaking practices.
- Allow students to earn credit:
  - For frequency and accuracy of responses.
  - For warm-up activities, partner practices, role-playing activities, and cooperative learning activities.
  - For attempted responses given in the target language, regardless of correctness.

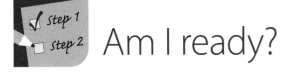

Am I ready?

☐ I have state and local **standards** and curriculum documents.

☐ I have developed units with a **backward design** process and have included clear goals and objectives.

☐ I have chosen a **lesson plan template** that will ensure I plan standards-based, engaging lessons, using a backward design process.

☐ I have well developed lessons for the first week that will keep my students **engaged** the entire period.

☐ I have **paced** my lessons appropriately and have a back-up plan for any remaining time in a period, to limit classroom management issues.

☐ I have planned the first week's lessons so students feel they are learning something new and exciting beginning on the first day.

☐ I have determined my **grading system** and am prepared to communicate it to parents, guardians, students and administrators.

☐ I have explained that I calculate points/percentages for each grade.

☐ I have clearly stated that I will/will not round up grades.

☐ I have explained how each grading period and final-year grade will be calculated. I have explained how much weight each category will have.

☐ I have included a copy of the rubric(s) I use for assessing student work.

☐ I have included the school district's policy for what constitutes: A, B, C, D, & F.

☐ I have checked all equipment to make sure everything is operational, and I know how to use the available equipment and resources.

☐ I am aware of the **digital tools and resources** available, and I have initial plans for effective integration of these tools.

☐ I have determined a policy for **cell phone** use (if applicable) as a part of my instructional and classroom management plan.

☐ I am aware of **IEP and 504 plans** for my students and have prepared for necessary accommodations.

☐ I have collaborated with colleagues, and I believe my immediate questions have been answered.

Reflection

What aspect of unit and lesson planning worked well?

What would I change for next year?

How would I change it?

What additional resources do I need to gather for next year?

Template A
Unit Plan Template

Lesson Design Overview

Theme/Topic	
Performance Range	
Essential Question	

Unit Goals

Summative Performance Tasks
Interpretive

Presentational	**Interpersonal**
Polished On demand	

Can-Do Statements	
Interpretive	
Presentational	
Interpersonal	

Supporting Functions	**Supporting Structures/Patterns**	**Priority Vocabulary**

Resources

Clementi, D., & Terrill, L. (2017). *The Keys to Planning for Learning: Effective Curriculum, Unit, and Lesson Design (Second Edition).* Alexandria, VA: ACTFL.

Template B

Lesson Plan Template

Performance Target		Grade		Date		Day in Unit		Minutes
Theme/Topic								
Essential Question								
Daily topic:								

STANDARDS	LESSON OBJECTIVES			
What are the communicative and cultural objectives for the lesson?	**Communication** *and* **Cultures**	*Which modes of communication will be addressed?*	Learners can:	
		☐ Interpersonal		
		☐ Interpretive		
		☐ Presentational		

Lesson Sequence	**Activity/Activities** What will learners do? What does the teacher do?	**Time** How many minutes will this segment take?	**Materials/Resources/ Technology** Be specific. What materials will you develop? What materials will you bring in from other sources?
Gain Attention / Activate Prior Knowledge			
Provide Input			
Elicit Performance / Provide Feedback			

Remember that the maximum attention span of the learner is approximately the age of the learner up to 20 minutes. The initial lesson cycle (gain attention/activate prior knowledge, provide input and elicit performance/provide feedback) would not take more than 20 minutes. Additional cycles (provide input and elicit performance/provide feedback) would be repeated as needed and the number of cycles would vary depending on the length of the class period.

Closure			
Enhance Retention & Transfer			
Reflection – Notes to Self	• What worked well? Why? • What didn't work? Why? • What changes would you make if you taught this lesson again?		

Template C
Simplified Lesson Plan Template

Simplified World Languages Lesson Plan

State Standards Objective(s):		
EQ or I Can Statement(s):		
Formative Assessments (to be distributed throughout the lesson; may also be guided/independent practice activities): Circle the mode(s): Interpretive Communication, Interpersonal Communication, Presentational Communication		
Activating Strategy/Bell Ringer:	**Teacher Role:**	**Student Role:**
Input/Model:	**Teacher Role:**	**Student Role:**
Guided Practice: Circle the mode(s): Interpretive Communication, Interpersonal Communication, Presentational Communication	**Teacher Role:**	**Student Role:**
Independent Practice: Circle the mode(s): Interpretive Communication, Interpersonal Communication, Presentational Communication	**Teacher Role:**	**Student Role:**
Closure/Summarizer:	**Teacher Role:**	**Student Role:**
Resources Needed:		

Template D | Example Lesson Plan

Simplified World Languages Lesson Plan – Example Chinese Lesson

State Standards Objective(s): Novice Mid/Interpretive: I can understand the meaning of memorized phrases and questions about familiar topics. Novice Mid/Interpersonal: Use memorized words and phrases to exchange information on familiar topics.		
EQ or I Can Statement(s): I can identify animals of the Chinese zodiac. I can ask and answer questions about pets.		
Formative Assessments (to be distributed throughout the lesson; may also be guided/independent practice activities): Peer interviews, two paired activities – see Guided/Independent Practice and Closure Circle the mode(s): ⟨Interpretive Communication⟩, ⟨Interpersonal Communication⟩, Presentational Communication		

Activating Strategy/Bell Ringer:	**Teacher Role:**	**Student Role:**
• Show pictures or a video of people with pets in China. Have students compare similarities and differences of pet-keeping culture in China and their own country with words and patterns they have, such as: 很喜欢, 爱, 有, etc.	• Show pictures/video.	• Use a Venn diagram to make note of differences/similarities they observe.
Input/Model:	**Teacher Role:**	**Student Role:**
• Use the Chinese Zodiac to present animal vocabulary. Ask students under which animal year they were born. Create a list with pictures on the board/screen of the animals. Ask students to add to the list with animals they saw in the video/pictures that aren't on the zodiac. Have students repeat the vocabulary while gesturing to represent the animal.	• Present vocabulary with visuals and gestures. • Ensure all are participating in vocabulary/gestures.	• Identify pets seen in video that aren't on zodiac. • Repeat vocabulary and gestures.
Guided Practice:	**Teacher Role:**	**Student Role:**
• Call out an animal name and students perform the gesture to show understanding. When they seem ready, show a gesture, and students call out the name. • Toss a soft globe to ask students if they have any of these animals as pets using the patterns: 你家有… (狗)吗? or, 你家有没有 • … (狗) ? Then, ask them how many (animals) do they have? 你有几只/条…? In between, recycle both patterns using third person pronouns: 他ta, 她ta: 他/她家有 (狗) 吗 ? 他/她家有几只/条… (狗) ? What kind of animal(s) does s/he have? How many? • To keep students' focus, ask others to report what a peer said in their answer. • As students become comfortable with the formulaic questions/answers, have students toss the globe to ask questions of peers. • Circle the mode(s): ⟨Interpretive Communication⟩, ⟨Interpersonal Communication⟩, Presentational Communication	• Lead vocabulary practice by calling out animal names, then showing gestures. • Ask questions, modeling the format and giving either/or answers as examples to help students answer. • Provide question stems/answers for students as needed.	• Show comprehension with gestures and saying animal names. • Answer questions and listen to peers' answers to be able to report what they said. • Lead the activity by tossing the globe and asking questions.

Continued on next page

Independent Practice:	**Teacher Role:**	**Student Role:**
• Have students interview each other about their pets. Provide a graphic organizer with question stems/answers and a place to record answers from four students. Have two students model the activity. Give students 8-10 minutes to circulate and interview four peers each. Afterward ask some students to report about their peers. • Have students work in pairs. Give pairs small bags with Chinese characters and animal pictures on individual pieces of paper. Have students match the pictures to characters, based on prior knowledge of character formation. Show correct matching on the screen and ask pairs on how many they were correct. Ask them to correct their matches before returning pieces to the bag. • Circle the mode(s): Interpretive Communication, Interpersonal Communication, Presentational Communication	• Provide graphic organizer and model the interview. Circulate during interviews to coach as needed and time the activity. Ask students to report about their peers answers. • Provide bags with Chinese characters and animal pictures. Circulate as pairs work together to guess the matches. Show correct matches. Ask how many had three correct, five correct, etc.	• Use the graphic organizer and question stems/sentence starters to ask and answer questions with peers. Talk with at least four peers. Report about another students' answers. • Work with a partner to identify the Chinese character for the animal names, based on knowledge of Chinese character formation.
Closure/Summarizer:	**Teacher Role:**	**Student Role:**
• Have students work in pairs. Provide picture flashcards of the animals. Name an animal and the students are to touch the picture. If ready, have a student or students lead the activity.	• Provide flashcard sets (could be student created). • Call out names of animals. • Choose students to lead.	• Participate in pairs. Try to be the first to touch the flashcard. Lead activity if asked or if volunteering to do so.

Resources Needed:
• Video/pictures of pets in China • Chinese zodiac • Picture and character cards for magnetic board or ready to display on screen • Graphic organizers for interview activity • Bags with characters/animal pictures • Sets of picture flashcards with zodiac animals/pets

Template E | Unit Design Reflection Checklist

To Do	Questions to Ask
Select the theme (based on local curriculum)	• What will be the context for the language?
Define the unit objectives (based on state curriculum/proficiency targets)	• What learning objectives will be met? • What will learners be able to DO (read, write, say, understand) in the language at the end of the unit? • What are the "Can-Do Statements" that will be addressed in the unit?
Develop the summative assessment	• How will I know learners met the unit objectives/learned the new language skills? • What evidence will learners have to show that aligns with the unit objectives? • How will this be graded?
Develop the daily lessons (includes activities and formative assessments)	• How will I help learners get to the end goal and be successful on the summative assessment? • How will I scaffold their learning? • How will I address various learning styles and higher order thinking skills? • How will I monitor their progress and provide feedback throughout the unit?

Identify/Locate/Create the resources	• What resources do I need that are readily available?
	• What do I need to create?
	  – Textbook resources?
	  – Digital devices and resources?
	  – Manipulatives and visuals?
	  – Examples of assessments?
	  – Rubrics?

Teach the unit	• How will I implement the overall plan and daily lessons? • Specifically, how will I introduce new vocabulary and structures in context? • How will I model and teach new activities? • How will I use comprehensible input to avoid use of English by me and students?
Reflect/Evaluate the unit	• What went well, and why? • What didn't work well, and why not? • What should be changed for next time? • Which activities should be repeated? • Which ones need to be changed or eliminated? • Were learners successful? Why or why not?

Template F | Lesson Design Reflection Checklist

To Do	Questions to Ask
Determine the subtopic of the unit (based on unit plan)	• Which part of the larger unit theme is to be addressed?
Define the language objectives (based on state curriculum/proficiency targets)	• Which state standards or objectives will be met? • What will learners be able to *do* (read, write, say, understand) in the language at the end of the lesson? • To which "can-do statements" does the lesson align?
Develop the formative assessments	• How will I know they are learning the new language and skills? • How will I provide feedback?
Determine the lesson activities	• How will I help them meet the language objectives for the day? • How will one activity lead to the next one? • How will I make the language relevant to learners and engage them in using the language for a meaningful purpose? • What specific questions will I ask or examples will I give? • What is the "bell ringer" activity? • What will be the closure/summarizer?
Identify/Locate/Create the resources	• What resources do I need that are readily available? What do I need to create? Textbook resources? On-line resources? Digital devices and resources? Manipulatives and visuals? Examples of final products? Rubrics?
Teach the lesson	• How will I implement the activities? • How will I transition from one to the next smoothly and quickly? • How will I model activities, give instructions, give explanations, and stay in the target language?
Evaluate the lesson	• What do the formative assessment activities tell me? • How does that affect the next lesson? • What went well, and what didn't? Why? • What do I need to adjust for next time?

Template G | Formative Assessment Task Template 1

High School

Formative Speaking/Writing Task (select one)
Level _____ – French/German/Spanish (select one)

Theme: (Select theme from local curriculum)

Topic: (Select topic from local curriculum)

Task Objective:

To … (Try to keep this short and refer to the necessary language functions. For example: To describe a weekend trip)

Task Description:

You are … (Create a scenario. At the end of the task description, put in bold the main thing the learner is to do.)

Minimum Requirements to Meet Expectations:

(Include …, Write …) (Try to list no more than 3–5 bullets)

Suggestions:

You may want to … (Add additional ideas that might exceed minimum expectations for the task. Be careful not to suggest something they cannot do. Inclusion of suggestions should earn points in the highest level on the rubric.)

Directions: You have _____ seconds to prepare and _____ seconds to speak. (speaking task)

You have _____ minutes to write a minimum of _____ sentences. (writing task)

Scoring Criteria: Level speaking/writing analytic rubric (chose one)

Say / Write (choose one) **as much as you can! Show off what you can do!**

(You may want to include here a graphic organizer for learners to use when doing the task.)

Optional:
Teacher Note(s)

(Suggestions for teachers on what to introduce to learners beforehand, what visuals to provide, etc.)

Template H

Example Formative Assessment Task

High School

Writing Task
Level 1 – French

Theme: Personal and Family Life

Topic: Clothing and Colors; Weather and Seasons; Interests and Leisure Activities

Task Objective: To describe weather, seasons, and related clothing and activities

Task Description: Your friend from Paris is coming to visit you in the winter. Your friend wants to know what the weather is like in the United States and what you wear. He/she also wants to know what you do for fun. Write your friend an email about the weather, appropriate clothing, and likely activities for February.

Minimum Requirements to Meet Expectations:
- Describe what the weather is like.
- Describe at least three clothing items to bring.
- Describe at least three activities you do.

Suggestions: You may want to ask your friend what he/she does in February.

Directions: You have 15 minutes to write as much as you can. Be sure to address the prompt. You may use the graphic organizer below to make notes before you begin writing.

Scoring Criteria: Level 1 writing analytic rubric

Write as much as you can! Show off what you can do!

Weather	Clothing	Activities

Template I

Example Integrated Performance Assessment (IPA)

High School

Thematically Organized Assessment (TOA)
French

TOA Title: *Il fait chaud! J'ai soif!*

Theme: Art of Well-Being

Level: Novice-Mid

TOA Overview: You and your friend are at your home, and it is a hot summer day; you are very thirsty. The two of you decide you want something refreshing to drink. You decide to look up French beverage recipes on the Internet. After you select two recipes, you talk about the weather, how thirsty you are, which beverage you would like to drink, and why. Then, you decide to create your own drink that would be helpful in such hot weather. You will write the recipe for your refreshing drink.

Thematically Organized Assessment (TOA)
French

Task Title: *Il fait chaud! J'ai soif!*

Theme: Art of Well-Being

Level: Novice-Mid

Focus Age Group: Ages 10–12

World-Readiness Standards Goals: Communication, Communities

Communicative Mode: Interpretive

Time Frame: One 30-minute class period

Description of Task: You and your friend are at your home, and it is a hot summer day; you are very thirsty. Both of you decide you want something refreshing to drink. You look up recipes on the Internet.

Materials Needed: Copies of attached comprehension guide.

Teacher Notes:
1. Describe the task to the students (see description above).
2. Explain the rubric (see attached).
3. Distribute comprehension guide (see attached).
4. Students complete comprehension guide.

Please Note: For original source of recipes, see website: http://www.recettes.qc.ca. Underneath the "*Recettes*" column, click on "*Boissons.*" Select the following recipes:
- *Lait frappé*
- *Limonade d'été*

Comprehension Guide

Nom _____

Il fait chaud! J'ai soif!

You and your friend are at your home and it's a hot summer day; you are very thirsty. Both of you decide you want something different to drink. You look up recipes on the Internet.

Recettes du Québec	**Recettes du Québec**
http://www.recettes.qc.ca	*http://www.recettes.qc.ca*
Lait frappé	**Limonade d'été**
Préparation: 15 minutes	*Préparation: 5 minutes*
Cuisson: 0 minutes	*Cuisson: 0 minutes*
Portions: 1	*Portions: 1*
Ingrédients	**Ingrédients**
¾ de tasse ou 2 grosses boules de crème glacé	*1 à 1½ jus de citron 1 tasse d'eau froide*
½ tasse de lait	*1 cuillère à thé de sucre (au goût)*
¼ cuillère à thé de vanille	
Méthode	**Méthode**
1. *Mélanger tous les ingrédients dans un mélangeur ou directement dans un grand verre!*	**1.** *Mélanger le jus de citron, le sucre et l'eau. Servir froid.*
Variante: Remplacer la crème glacé à la vanille par une saveur de votre choix (fraise, chocolat).	*Recette envoyée par: Bernard*

Circle the words that are mentioned in the two recipes.

First Recipe: *Lait frappé*

Milk	Small	Chocolate	Vanilla	Ingredients	Ice cream
Milkshake	Mix	Big	Banana	Glass	Ice

Second Recipe: *Limonade d'été*

Lemonade	Cup	Lime	Cold	Lemon	Sugar
Orange	Mix	Hot	Water	Milk	Juice

What are the names of these two drinks? _____

What do you think is the difference between "*Préparation*" and "*Cuisson*"?

_____

_____

Interpretive Mode Rubric: A Continuum of Performance

CRITERIA	Exceeds Expectations	Meets Expectations		Does Not Meet Expectations
	Accomplished Comprehension	Strong Comprehension	Minimal Comprehension	Limited Comprehension
LITERAL COMPREHENSION				
Word Recognition	Identifies all key words appropriately within context of the text.	Identifies majority of key words appropriately within context of the text.	Identifies half of key words appropriately within the context of the text.	Identifies a few key words appropriately within the context of the text.
Main idea detection	Identifies the complete main idea(s) of the text.	Identifies the key parts of the main idea(s) of the text but misses some elements.	Identifies some part of the main idea(s) of the text.	May identify some ideas from the text but they do not represent main idea(s).
Supporting detail detection	Identifies all supporting details in the text and accurately provides information from the text to explain these details.	Identifies the majority of supporting details in the text and provides information from the text to explain some of these details.	Identifies some supporting details in the text and may provide limited information from the text to explain these details. Or identifies the majority of supporting details but is unable to provide information from the text to explain these details.	Identifies a few supporting details in the text but may be unable to provide information from the text to explain these details.
INTERPRETIVE COMPREHENSION				
Organizational features	Identifies the organizational feature(s) of the text and provides an appropriate rationale.	Identifies the organizational feature(s) of the text; rationale misses some key points.	Identifies in part the organizational feature(s) of the text; rationale may miss some key points. Or identifies the organizational feature(s) but rationale is not provided.	Attempts to identify the organizational feature(s) of the text but is not successful.
Guessing meaning from context	Infers meaning of unfamiliar words and phrases in the text. Inferences are accurate.	Infers meaning of unfamiliar words and phrases in the text. Most inferences are plausible, although some may not be accurate.	Infers meaning of unfamiliar words and phrases in the text. Most inferences are plausible, although many are not accurate.	Inferences of meaning of unfamiliar words and phrases are largely inaccurate or lacking.
Inferences (Reading/listening/viewing between the lines)	Infers and interprets the text's meaning in a highly plausible manner.	Infers and interprets the text's meaning in a partially complete and/or partially plausible manner.	Makes a few plausible inferences regarding the text's meaning.	Inferences and interpretations of the text's meaning are largely incomplete and/or not plausible.
Author's perspective	Identifies the author's perspective and provides a detailed justification.	Identifies the author's perspective and provides a justification.	Identifies the author's perspective but justification is either inappropriate or incomplete.	Unable to identify the author's perspective.
Cultural perspectives	Identifies cultural perspectives/norms accurately. Provides a detailed connection of cultural products/practices to perspectives.	Identifies some cultural perspectives/norms accurately. Connects cultural products/practices to perspectives.	Identifies some cultural perspectives/norms accurately. Provides a minimal connection of cultural products/ practices to perspectives.	Identification of cultural perspectives/norms is mostly superficial or lacking, and/or connection of cultural practices/products to perspectives is superficial or lacking.

* The Interpretive Rubric is designed to show the continuum of performance for both literal and interpretive comprehension for language learners regardless of language level. See *Implementing Integrated Performance Assessment*, Chapter 2, for suggestions on how to use this rubric to assign a score or grade.

Adair-Hauck, B., Glisan, E. W., & Troyan, F. J. (2013) *Implementing Integrated Performance Assessment*. Alexandria, VA: ACTFL.

Task Title: *Il fait chaud! J'ai soif!*

Theme: Art of Well-Being

Level: Novice-Mid

Focus Age Group: Ages 10–12

World-Readiness Standards Goals: Communication, Connections, Communities

Communicative Mode: Interpersonal

Time Frame: Depending on the number of students, one may need one or two 30-minute classes.

Description of Task: You and your friend are at your home and it's a hot summer day. Ask and answer questions of each other in order to decide which drink you would like to try. Be sure to address the topics below in your conversation. Be sure that both of you ask and answer questions as a part of the conversation, responding to one another appropriately.

1. Weather
2. Thirst
3. Preference for something to drink
4. Reason for preference

Materials Needed: None

Teacher Notes: During prior lessons, students will have learned to talk about the weather and whether or not someone is thirsty.

1. Describe the task to the students (see description above).
2. Explain the rubric (see below).
3. Model the conversation with a student.
4. Teacher should pair students.
5. Students talk with partners.
6. Teacher evaluates using scoring rubric.

Interpersonal Mode Rubric – Novice Learner

CRITERIA	Exceeds Expectations	Meets Expectations		Does Not Meet Expectations
Language Function Language tasks the speaker is able to handle in a consistent, comfortable, sustained, and spontaneous manner	Creates with language by combining and recombining known elements; is able to express personal meaning in a basic way. Handles successfully a number of uncomplicated communicative tasks in straightforward social situations, primarily in concrete exchanges and topics necessary for survival in target-language cultures.	Uses mostly memorized language with some attempts to create. Handles a limited number of uncomplicated communicative tasks involving topics related to basic personal information and some activities, preferences, and immediate needs.	Uses memorized language only, familiar language.	Has no real functional ability.
Text Type Quantity and organization of language discourse (continuum: word - phrase - sentence - connected sentences - paragraph - extended discourse)	Uses simple sentences and some strings of sentences.	Uses some simple sentences and memorized phrases.	Uses words, phrases, chunks of language, and lists.	Uses isolated words.
Communication Strategies Quality of engagement and interactivity; how one participates in the conversation and advances it; strategies for negotiating meaning in the face of breakdown of communication	Responds to direct questions and requests for information. Asks a few appropriate questions, but is primarily reactive. May try to restate in the face of miscommunication.	Responds to basic direct questions and requests for information. Asks a few formulaic questions but is primarily reactive. May clarify by repeating and/or substituting different words.	Responds to a limited number of formulaic questions. May use repetition or resort to English.	Is unable to participate in a true conversational exchange.
Comprehensibility Who can understand this person's language? Can this person be understood only by sympathetic listeners used to interacting with non-natives? Can a native speaker unaccustomed to non-native speech understand this speaker?	Is generally understood by those accustomed to interacting with non-natives, although repetition or rephrasing may be required.	Is understood with occasional difficulty by those accustomed to interacting with non-natives, although repetition or rephrasing may be required.	Is understood, although often with difficulty, by those accustomed to interacting with non-natives.	Most of what is said may be unintelligible or understood only with repetition.
Language Control Grammatical accuracy, appropriate vocabulary, degree of fluency	Is most accurate when producing simple sentences in present time. Pronunciation, vocabulary, and syntax are strongly influenced by the native language. Accuracy decreases as language becomes more complex.	Is most accurate with memorized language, including phrases. Accuracy decreases when creating and trying to express personal meaning.	Accuracy is limited to memorized words. Accuracy may decrease when attempting to communicate beyond the word level.	Has little accuracy, even with memorized words.

Adair-Hauck, B., Glisan, E. W., & Troyan, F. J. (2013) *Implementing Integrated Performance Assessment.* Alexandria, VA: ACTFL.

Task Title: *Il fait chaud! J'ai soif!*

Theme: Art of Well-Being

Level: Novice-Mid

Focus Age Group: Ages 10–12

World-Readiness Standards Goals: Communication, Culture, Connections

Communicative Mode: Presentational

Time Frame: Approximately 30 minutes

Description of Task: It is a very hot summer day, and you decide to make yourself something cold to drink. You want to get creative and fix something other than what you found online. Using some culturally appropriate ingredients, write your own recipe for a refreshing drink.*

- Include all necessary ingredients.
- Include amounts for the ingredients.
- Include at least one culturally appropriate ingredient (something native to a Francophone country).
- Provide instructions for the steps in the recipe.
- You may want to include an illustration.

*Note: If you have not included culturally authentic food in previous lessons, either leave this part out of the instructions, or provide another activity that helps students gain some knowledge to be able to address this component.

Teacher Notes:

1. Describe the task to the students (see description above).
2. Explain the rubric.
3. Students write recipes and turn them in (or submit electronically)

Presentational Mode Rubric – Novice Learner

CRITERIA	Exceeds Expectations	Meets Expectations		Does Not Meet Expectations
Language Function Language tasks the speaker/writer is able to handle in a consistent, comfortable, sustained, and spontaneous manner	Creates with language by combining and recombining known elements; is able to express personal meaning in a basic way. Handles successfully a number of uncomplicated communicative tasks and topics necessary for survival in target-language cultures.	Uses mostly memorized language with some attempts to create. Handles a limited number of uncomplicated communicative tasks involving topics related to basic personal information and some activities, preferences, and immediate needs.	Uses memorized language only, familiar language.	Has no real functional ability.
Text Type Quantity and organization of language discourse (continuum: word - phrase - sentence - connected sentences - paragraph - extended discourse)	Uses simple sentences and some strings of sentences.	Uses some simple sentences and memorized phrases.	Uses words, phrases, chunks of language, and lists.	Uses isolated words.
Impact Clarity, organization, and depth of presentation; degree to which presentation maintains attention and interest of audience	Presented in a clear and organized manner. Presentation illustrates originality, rich details, and an unexpected feature that captures interest and attention of audience.	Presented in a clear and organized manner. Presentation illustrates originality and features rich details, visuals, and/or organization of the text to maintain audience's attention and/or interest.	Presented in a clear and organized manner. Some effort to maintain audience's attention through visuals, organization of the text, and/or details.	Presentation may be either unclear or unorganized. Minimal to no effort to maintain audience's attention.
Comprehensibility Who can understand this person's language? Can this person be understood only by sympathetic interlocutors used to the language of non-natives? Can a native speaker unaccustomed to the speaking/writing of non-natives understand this speaker/writer?	Is generally understood by those accustomed to the speaking/writing of non-natives, although additional effort may be required.	Is understood with occasional difficulty by those accustomed to the speaking/writing of non-natives, although additional effort may be required.	Is understood, although often with difficulty, by those accustomed to the speaking/writing of non-natives.	Most of spoken/written language may be unintelligible or understood only with additional effort.
Language Control Grammatical accuracy, appropriate vocabulary, degree of fluency	Is most accurate when producing simple sentences in present time. Pronunciation, vocabulary, and syntax are strongly influenced by the native language. Accuracy decreases as language becomes more complex.	Is most accurate with memorized language, including phrases. Accuracy decreases when creating and trying to express personal meaning.	Accuracy is limited to memorized words. Accuracy may decrease when attempting to communicate beyond the word level.	Has little accuracy even with memorized words.

Adair-Hauck, B., Glisan, E. W., & Troyan, F. J. (2013) *Implementing Integrated Performance Assessment.* Alexandria, VA: ACTFL.

Template J

Example Integrated Performance Assessment (IPA)

Thematically Organized Assessment (TOA)
Spanish

TOA Title: *Una Casa en España*

Theme: What Makes My House a Home

Level: Intermediate–Low

TOA Overview:

What an experience! Your family is moving to Spain for a year. Your mother will be working on a special project for her company, and everyone will spend the year abroad. A packet of information for the move arrives in the mail. Your mother is confused by some of the documents and asks you to help her interpret the information, because you have been learning Spanish since elementary school.

One of her first concerns is housing. You scan online real estate ads to find appropriate places to live. After looking at the options, you talk with your friends about the pros and cons of the options and come to a decision about which one is best.

Your family bought a home in Barcelona and everyone is looking forward to the experience of living abroad. Once you arrive in the country, you help your parents communicate ideas to the decorator. You write a detailed description of your family's likes and dislikes, the amenities you need and want, and you make suggestions about furniture and accessories for the house. You even draw a layout of the house and label the items you want in each room.

Task Title: *Una Casa en España*

Theme: What Makes My House a Home

Level: Intermediate–Low

Focus Age Group: 13+

World-Readiness Standards Goals: Communication, Cultures

Communicative Mode: Interpretive

Time frame: One class period (40 minutes)

Description of Task: After searching the Internet for real estate ads for houses and apartments to rent or buy in Spain, you find a few places that look interesting. To present the information to your family, you scan the ads carefully and jot down important information.

Materials Needed: Websites and Interpretive Task sheets

http://www.spainhouses.net/es/index.php

http://www.fotocasa.es/index.aspx

Teacher Notes: Scan the websites listed above to find appropriate real estate ads for the task. Choose at least three to five homes that students might use to complete the Comprehension Guide. You might print out ads or allow students to search online.

Interpretive Activity Sheet

Una Casa en España

I. After scanning the ads, you organize the information about the houses and apartments by filling in a chart about each residence.

Name/ Number of Residence	Type of Residence	Location	Size	Rooms	Special Features

II. Compare your residence to one of the Spanish residences:

_____

_____

_____

_____

III. Some of the words were unfamiliar. You made guesses about the meanings.

1. *inmobilaria* _____

2. *particulares* _____

3. *en alquiler* _____

4. *piso* _____

5. *planta baja* _____

VI. Answer the following questions by providing as many reasons as you can. Your responses may be in English.

_____

_____

_____

_____

VII. Which house/apartment do you prefer and why? Use details from the ads to support your answers.

_____

_____

_____

_____

VIII. Do you believe that your family will enjoy their stay in Spain? Explain.

_____

_____

_____

_____

Interpretive Mode Rubric: A Continuum of Performance

CRITERIA	Exceeds Expectations	Meets Expectations		Does Not Meet Expectations
	Accomplished Comprehension	Strong Comprehension	Minimal Comprehension	Limited Comprehension
LITERAL COMPREHENSION				
Word recognition	Identifies all key words appropriately within context of the text.	Identifies majority of key words appropriately within context of the text.	Identifies half of key words appropriately within the context of the text.	Identifies a few key words appropriately within the context of the text.
Main idea detection	Identifies the complete main idea(s) of the text.	Identifies the key parts of the main idea(s) of the text but misses some elements.	Identifies some part of the main idea(s) of the text.	May identify some ideas from the text but they do not represent the main idea(s).
Supporting detail detection	Identifies all supporting details in the text and accurately provides information from the text to explain these details.	Identifies the majority of supporting details in the text and provides information from the text to explain some of these details.	Identifies some supporting details in the text and may provide limited information from the text to explain these details. Or identifies the majority of supporting details but is unable to provide information from the text to explain these details.	Identifies a few supporting details in the text but may be unable to provide information from the text to explain these details.
INTERPRETIVE COMPREHENSION				
Organizational features	Identifies the organizational feature(s) of the text and provides an appropriate rationale.	Identifies the organizational feature(s) of the text; rationale misses some key points.	Identifies in part the organizational feature(s) of the text; rationale may miss some key points. Or identifies the organizational feature(s) but rationale is not provided.	Attempts to identify the organizational feature(s) of the text but is not successful.
Guessing meaning from context	Infers meaning of unfamiliar words and phrases in the text. Inferences are accurate.	Infers meaning of unfamiliar words and phrases in the text. Most of the inferences are plausible although some may not be accurate.	Infers meaning of unfamiliar words and phrases in the text. Most of the inferences are plausible although many are not accurate.	Inferences of meaning of unfamiliar words and phrases are largely inaccurate or lacking.
Inferences (reading/ listening/viewing between the lines)	Infers and interprets the text's meaning in a highly plausible manner.	Infers and interprets the text's meaning in a partially complete and/or partially plausible manner.	Makes a few plausible inferences regarding the text's meaning.	Inferences and interpretations of the text's meaning are largely incomplete and/or not plausible.
Author's perspective	Identifies the author's perspective and provides a detailed justification.	Identifies the author's perspective and provides a justification.	Identifies the author's perspective but justification is either inappropriate or incomplete.	Unable to identify the author's perspective.
Cultural perspectives	Identifies cultural perspectives/norms accurately. Provides a detailed connection of cultural products/practices to perspectives.	Identifies some cultural perspectives/norms accurately. Connects cultural products/ practices to perspectives.	Identifies some cultural perspectives/norms accurately. Provides a minimal connection of cultural products/ practices to perspectives.	Identification of cultural perspectives/norms is mostly superficial or lacking. And/ or connection of cultural practices/ products to perspectives is superficial or lacking.

* The Interpretive Rubric is designed to show the continuum of performance for both literal and interpretive comprehension for language learners regardless of language level. See *Implementing Integrated Performance Assessment*, Chapter 2, for suggestions on how to use this rubric to assign a score or grade.

Adair-Hauck, B., Glisan, E. W., & Troyan, F. J. (2013) *Implementing Integrated Performance Assessment*. Alexandria, VA: ACTFL.

Task Title: *Una Casa en España*

Theme: What Makes My House a Home

Level: Intermediate–Low

Focus Age Group: 13+

World-Readiness Standards Goals: Communication, Comparison

Communicative Mode: Interpersonal

Time Frame: 40 minutes

Description of Task: Now that you have looked at various options for housing, you need to decide what to recommend to your family. Talk with your partner about the choices and decide which will be best. In your partners ask each other questions about the families' needs and preferences. Discuss how your two favorite options address those needs and preferences.

Interpersonal Mode Rubric – Intermediate Learner

CRITERIA	Exceeds Expectations	Meets Expectations		Does Not Meet Expectations
Language Function Language tasks the speaker is able to handle in a consistent, comfortable, sustained, and spontaneous manner	Handles successfully uncomplicated tasks and social situations requiring exchange of basic information related to work, school, recreation, particular interests, and areas of competence. Narrates and describes in all major time frames, although not consistently.	Creates with language by combining and recombining known elements; ability to express own meaning expands in quantity and quality. Handles successfully a variety of uncomplicated communicative tasks in straightforward social situations, primarily in concrete exchanges and topics necessary for survival in target-language cultures. These exchanges include personal information related to self, interests, and personal preferences, as well as physical and social needs such as food, shopping, and travel.	Creates with language by combining and recombining known elements; is able to express personal meaning in a basic way. Handles successfully a number of uncomplicated communicative tasks in straightforward social situations, primarily in concrete exchanges and topics necessary for survival in target-language cultures.	Has no real functional ability.
Text Type Quantity and organization of language discourse (continuum: word - phrase - sentence - connected sentences - paragraph - extended discourse)	Uses mostly connected sentences and some paragraph-like discourse.	Uses strings of sentences, with some complex sentences (dependent clauses).	Uses simple sentences and some strings of sentences.	Uses some simple sentences and memorized phrases.
Communication Strategies Quality of engagement and interactivity; how one participates in the conversation and advances it; strategies for negotiating meaning in the face of breakdown of communication	Converses with ease and confidence when dealing with routine tasks and social situations. May clarify by paraphrasing.	Responds to direct questions and requests for information. Asks a variety of questions to obtain simple information but tends to function reactively. May clarify by restating.	Responds to direct questions and requests for information. Asks a few appropriate questions, but is primarily reactive. May try to restate in the face of miscommunication.	Responds to basic direct questions and requests for information. Asks a few formulaic questions but is primarily reactive. May clarify by repeating and/or substituting different words.
Comprehensibility Who can understand this person's language? Can this person be understood only by sympathetic listeners used to interacting with non-natives? Can a native speaker unaccustomed to non-native speech understand this speaker?	Is generally understood by those unaccustomed to interacting with non-natives, although interference from another language may be evident and gaps in communication may occur.	Is generally understood by those accustomed to interacting with non-natives.	Is generally understood by those accustomed to interacting with non-natives, although repetition or rephrasing may be required.	Is understood with occasional difficulty by those accustomed to interacting with non-natives, although repetition or rephrasing may be required.
Language Control Grammatical accuracy, appropriate vocabulary, degree of fluency	Demonstrates significant quantity and quality of Intermediate-level language. When attempting to perform Advanced-level tasks, there is breakdown in one or more of the following areas: the ability to narrate and describe, use of paragraph-length discourse, fluency, breadth of vocabulary.	Demonstrates significant quantity and quality of Intermediate-level language. Accuracy and/or fluency decreases when attempting to handle topics at the Advanced level or as language becomes more complex.	Is most accurate when producing simple sentences in present time. Pronunciation, vocabulary, and syntax are strongly influenced by the native language. Accuracy decreases as language becomes more complex.	Is most accurate with memorized language, including phrases. Accuracy decreases when creating and trying to express personal meaning.

Adair-Hauck, B., Glisan, E. W., & Troyan, F. J. (2013) *Implementing Integrated Performance Assessment.* Alexandria, VA: ACTFL.

Task Title: *Una Casa en España*

Theme: What Makes My House a Home

Level: Intermediate–Low

Focus Age Group: 13+

World-Readiness Standards Goals: Communication, Cultures, Comparisons

Communicative Mode: Presentational

Time Frame: One class period (40 minutes)

Description of Task: Your family has arrived in Spain. Your parents are meeting with a decorator and need your help once again. You write a detailed description of your family members' likes and dislikes, the furniture you want and need in each room, and you make suggestions about furniture and accessories for the house. You may even draw or create a layout of the house to accompany the description.

Presentational Mode Rubric – Intermediate Learner

CRITERIA	Exceeds Expectations	Meets Expectations		Does Not Meet Expectations
Language Function Language tasks the speaker/writer is able to handle in a consistent, comfortable, sustained, and spontaneous manner	Handles successfully uncomplicated tasks and social situations requiring exchange of basic information related to work, school, recreation, particular interests, and areas of competence. Narrates and describes in all major time frames, although not consistently.	Creates with language by combining and recombining known elements; ability to express own meaning expands in quantity and quality. Handles successfully a variety of uncomplicated communicative tasks and topics necessary for survival in target-language cultures. These exchanges include personal information related to self, interests, and personal preferences, as well as physical and social needs such as food, shopping, and travel.	Creates with language by combining and recombining known elements; is able to express personal meaning in a basic way. Handles successfully a number of uncomplicated communicative tasks and topics necessary for survival in target-language cultures.	Has no real functional ability.
Text Type Quantity and organization of language discourse (continuum: word - phrase - sentence - connected sentences - paragraph - extended discourse)	Uses mostly connected sentences and some paragraph-like discourse.	Uses strings of sentences, with some complex sentences (dependent clauses).	Uses simple sentences and some strings of sentences.	Uses some simple sentences and memorized phrases.
Impact Clarity, organization, and depth of presentation; degree to which presentation maintains attention and interest of audience	Presented in a clear and organized manner. Presentation illustrates originality, rich details, and an unexpected feature that captures interest and attention of audience.	Presented in a clear and organized manner. Presentation illustrates originality and features rich details, visuals, and/or organization of the text to maintain audience's attention and/ or interest.	Presented in a clear and organized manner. Some effort to maintain audience's attention through visuals, organization of the text, and/or details.	Presentation may be either unclear or unorganized. Minimal to no effort to maintain audience's attention.
Comprehensibility Who can understand this person's language? Can this person be understood only by sympathetic interlocutors used to the language of non-natives? Can a native speaker unaccustomed to the speaking/ writing of non-natives understand this speaker/writer?	Is generally understood by those unaccustomed to the speaking/writing of non-natives, although interference from another language may be evident and gaps in comprehension may occur.	Is generally understood by those accustomed to the speaking/writing of non-natives.	Is generally understood by those accustomed to interacting with non-natives, although additional effort may be required.	Is understood with occasional difficulty by those accustomed to the speaking/writing of non-natives, although additional effort may be required.
Language Control Grammatical accuracy, appropriate vocabulary, degree of fluency	Demonstrates significant quantity and quality of Intermediate-level language. When attempting to perform Advanced-level tasks, there is breakdown in one or more of the following areas: the ability to narrate and describe, use of paragraph-length discourse, fluency, breadth of vocabulary.	Demonstrates significant quantity and quality of Intermediate-level language. Accuracy and/or fluency decreases when attempting to handle topics at the Advanced level or as language becomes more complex.	Is most accurate when producing simple sentences in present time. Pronunciation, vocabulary, and syntax are strongly influenced by the native language. Accuracy decreases as language becomes more complex.	Is most accurate with memorized language, including phrases. Accuracy decreases when creating and trying to express personal meaning.

Adair-Hauck, B., Glisan, E. W., & Troyan, F. J. (2013) *Implementing Integrated Performance Assessment*. Alexandria, VA: ACTFL.

Successful Activity Checklist

(Adapted with permission from David Jahner)

Use the following checklist to help determine whether or not an activity is likely to be designed for success. Remember that student use of the target language is the most important overall component to consider!

		Guiding Questions	YES	NO
L **A** **N** **G** **U** **A** **G** **E**	**P**ace	• Is the estimated time frame for the activity appropriate? • Is there a payback for the time spent?		
	Relevant	• Does the content of the activity relate to learners and keep their interest?		
	Active	• Is there opportunity for movement in the activity? • Are all learners involved with the language?		
	Challenge	• Does the activity challenge learners without going beyond what they are able to do? • Does it involve more than the Understand/Remember levels of thinking?		
	Think	• Does the activity require learners to use the target language in a meaningful way?		
	Integrate	• Does the activity incorporate the current theme/unit of study? • Or potentially another content area?		
	Clear	• Are the instructions for the activity clear? • Have you provided a clear model? • Have you conducted "pre" activities to prepare students? • Do learners understand how they will be assessed?		
	Encourage	• Does the activity lead to learner success and promote the use of the target language?		
Is the target language the activity's primary focus?				

Chapter 3 | How Do I Prepare?

Now that you've thought about the planning process, it's time to address the things that help make those plans work:

- How will I deal with classroom management?
- How will I establish an environment conducive to learning?
- How should I communicate with parents?

These are all important questions to consider for a successful year. You are not supposed to automatically know all the answers as a new teacher. This chapter will address these and other related questions. As you consider these topics, remember to ask colleagues for their tips and tricks as well! There are templates and examples at the end of the chapter to further help you.

Classroom Management

If you are having classroom management problems, ask yourself:

- When are most issues occurring? At the beginning of class, the end of class, or during transitions?
- Do I make my expectations clear, or are students trying to guess what is on my mind?
- Do I give the students too much time to complete a particular assignment?
- Do I plan for effective transitions?
- Are my lessons interesting and relevant?
- Do my students understand why they are doing a particular activity?
- Have I changed activities often enough during a class period?
- Are my lesson objectives clearly stated and posted where students can see them?
- Are my students saying they hate "busy work"?
- Am I consistent in implementing classroom rules?
- Do students consider me a figure of authority or a friend?
- Do I follow through with consequences for students?
- Have I earned the respect of my students?
- Do I follow my own rules?

Many veteran educators have learned that when they use well-written lessons with a variety of activities, they have fewer classroom management issues. Learners want to know what they are going to learn today and whether it will be important down the road. Always explain the big picture to students and let them know how today's lesson fits into that program.

> ✓ Be prepared! Knowing what's coming next and having your materials ready is important for effective classroom management.

Using the *NCSSFL-ACTFL Can-Do Statements* is one way to help students understand the purpose behind their learning. Emphasizing student responsibilities and holding them accountable for participation can also help with management. (Example templates for these topics are at the end of the chapter.)

Another key to classroom management is setting the stage for respect. As long as there is mutual respect, and students see you as the authority figure, not a peer, then the structure of the class should be obvious. If you explain the consequence of breaking a class rule and then do not follow through with students who do, you will lose the respect of your class. It is sometimes difficult to reprimand a "good" student, but if you don't treat every student the same way, you could face a rebellion later on. Students want teachers to be fair. They often do not object to the rules, but they will be quick to lose trust in teachers who let some students get away with things that others cannot.

Classroom Rules

It is customary, and often a school policy, to post rules in conspicuous places for all students to see. Keep in mind that the bottom line for classroom management is to make every minute count. When learners are engaged in the lesson and not bored, classroom management issues are less likely to occur.

Additionally, consistency is key. If you say there will be a consequence for certain actions, there must be one and it must be consistent. When developing and posting rules, keep a positive classroom atmosphere. It is easy to write your classroom rules with "Do not" or "NOT allowed." Rules are much more effective if presented in a positive manner, such as "Be respectful and considerate of others" and "Come prepared to learn." Avoid the word "not."

Les Règles
RESPECTER
PARTICIPER
LEVER LA MAIN

Example of very simple rules in the target language
(Respect, Participate, Raise your hand)

Limit your list to about five basic rules. A lengthy list is overwhelming, and students may feel they can do nothing right. This is a case when less is more. Rules are typically posted in English, although they could be in the target language if they are very simply stated and cognates and visuals are used. (A rules template is at the end of this chapter.)

Things to keep in mind regarding rules include:

- *List only rules you know you will enforce.* If you are inconsistent in enforcing your rules, students will learn quickly that it's not important to follow them.
- *Be sure your rules and practices align with school rules.* For example, if a school rule says students can't wear hats inside, then you have to enforce that, regardless of whether you agree with it. Not doing so sends mixed messages to students.
- *Teach routines and procedures.* The establishment of these means fewer students will be off task. Establish set routines for entering and leaving class, and take the time to teach those routines.
- Plan your consequences for rule infractions *before* school starts, not in the middle of an infraction.
- Discuss your rules with your school's administrators, and make sure they will support you before you ever send a student to the office for breaking a rule.
- Some teachers even involve the students in the development of the class rules, and therefore have more ownership from the students in the management of the class.
- Students also find it interesting to investigate school or classroom rules in schools in target-language countries. This is a great way to involve them in the rule-setting process in an authentic way. Have learners identify what the expected behavior would look like, as well as the types of behaviors that would not follow the rules or guidelines.

Seating Arrangements

Since communication is a key component of language learning, your seating arrangement should facilitate interaction. Think of ways you can group students so the environment is still conducive to individual activities. Some teachers arrange their desks in rows, because they want to minimize talking at inappropriate times and limit cheating. Straight rows will accomplish this goal, but if you want students to practice with a partner, students will be twisting in their seats while trying to engage their partners. Also, it's easy for students to disengage while talking to the back of their classmates' heads.

Instead of inhibiting productive conversation, rethink how you can keep students on task and involved in the lesson; for example, by changing activities often and giving students more opportunities to use language in problem-solving. Try changing the seating arrangement at each grading period. You can also tell students it is a privilege to sit next to their friends, and if they talk at inappropriate times they will lose that seating privilege.

✅ Ask colleagues for suggestions about seating arrangements and visit other classrooms to see examples. Ask for management tips and tricks when seating students in groups and pairs.

Once you have established order in the class, arrange your students' desks in one of the following arrangements:

- *Horseshoe:* In this arrangement, students are able to see the faces of most of the students in the class and can start conversations easily when asked to do so.
- *Tables or groups of four desks:* In this formation, you can get groups of 4 to 6 to work together and discuss a topic or break into sub groups. For assessment purposes you may want to consider cover sheets or manila folders to set up mock cubicles.
- *Paired grouping:* Students are already paired with a partner. (This is ideal for tasks requiring partners throughout the lesson.)
- *Half and half:* Have half the class facing the other half. Now students will be able to look at half the class when asking and answering questions and can also work on partner drills with the person next to them.
- *Flexible seating:* This may include options for students other than traditional desks, such as tall tables at which students can stand, or large exercise balls as seats. If you use flexible seating, you may need to teach students to choose their seating options responsibly.

Student Names

One of your major challenges the first month of school will be to learn approximately 150 (or more) student names and faces. Learning names is extremely important to begin to build relationships with students, as well as for classroom management. Finding a method that works for you requires some experimentation. Some language teachers ask students to pick a name common to the target language—but this can create more stress during the first month of school, because the names have now doubled to 300! Here are some methods experienced teachers use:

- On your seating chart, place students alphabetically by *first* name instead of last name. Proponents of this method say it is easier to remember the first name this way.
- Ask students what their favorite activities are, and then group them by activity. If you have students with the same name, this helps you identify which one you are looking for. Also, you probably will remember what a student's favorite activity grouping is. This can be helpful when you want to inquire about their interests. Your

students will be impressed that you remember what they like to do.

- Have students decorate table tent cards bearing their names, and keep them in place for at least the first month. Let students decorate their tent cards in ways that demonstrate their special interests. That can also elicit dialogue in class.
- Place your seating chart where you can see it, but where students cannot. Ask a question or give a prompt first before naming students. Then, for a response or "volunteer," intentionally call on students by name to help you commit the names to memory.
- Play a name game as a warm-up at the start of each class period for the first week of school. Remember that the students may not know each other well, so such activities can help them learn names and build rapport with one another.
- Have students write their names and learning goals on an index card. Using an extra-large binger clip, attach all of the index cards for the students who sit at a particular desk to that desk. Have the students change the card on top to theirs at the beginning of each class. This reminds students of their goals and provides an easy way to see names as you circulate around the room.

Dress for Success

Many young teachers may be inclined to identify with the students they teach. After all, they are relatively close in age to students, especially those in high school upper-level classes. You must keep in mind, however, that you are a professional in charge of many students in a classroom. You must firmly establish that role in every way.

Like it or not, your work attire is a major definer of roles of teachers and students. If you come to work in casual clothing, such as jeans and a t-shirt, you are sure to look like most of your students, and it will be hard for them to regard you as an authority figure.

> ✅ You are an adult, an authority figure, and a professional. Look like one.

Some school districts have dress policies for teachers, but if there is no policy, you must think carefully about what your physical appearance will tell students in the class. The message should be, "I am in charge." If your school has a "dress down Friday," ask more experienced colleagues for dress code tips before showing up in shorts and a tank top. Here are a couple of tips for dressing for success:

- Definitely dress your best for parent conferences, Back-to-School Night, and award presentations. This sends a message to parents that the teacher is a professional and expects to be treated as such.
- Wear slacks, tucked-in shirts, skirts and/or dresses, and appropriate shoes. (Ties for men are required in some schools). It is best to ask your administrator.
- Definitely avoid casual wear: flip-flops, short skirts, shorts, tank tops or pants showing underwear, midriff, cleavage, jeans with holes and tears, see-through clothing, etc.
- Some schools have spirit days to support an activity or sporting event. Ask veteran teachers what the administration allows before arriving in inappropriate attire.
- Holiday attire and/or costumes may be permitted by some school districts, but banned by others, especially if the clothing has religious overtones. It is always best to ask first.

Creating a Language- and Culture-Rich Environment

There are two camps regarding classroom décor and the physical environment: (1) teachers who love decorating walls and bulletin boards, and (2) those who lack the creative confidence to design organized environments that will provide additional instructional resources for learners. If you feel challenged in this area, here are some suggestions for things to display:

- *Post material by grading period, semester, or entire year.*
- *Address thematic units in more than one level and/or language (if you have more than one preparation).* You could list all themes you will cover for that year by level and/or language (especially if you teach more than one level or language).
- *Post items that catch learners' attention and are informative.*
- *Post student work.* This is a great way to use bulletin board space while featuring your students' creative work.

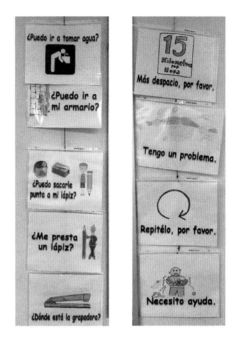

Key classroom expressions in the target language.

- *Make displays a low-maintenance tool.* Have students or members of a language club create a bulletin board or display and maintain it.
- *Create a collage of everyday material.* This may include food and drink labels, advertisements, coasters, candy wrappers, empty food containers, CD covers, newspaper headlines, magazine covers, and souvenirs students bring in as evidence of products made or consumed in a particular country, plus notices of current events and cultural information.
- *Build a display of key classroom questions/expressions with pictures attached.* This will remind all learners to stay in the target language no matter what level of instruction is taught, so they will take risks and start using the expressions in their writings. Put sentences, commands and questions on the bulletin board in the target language, such as "I need _____." "May I go to the bathroom?" "I don't understand." "Please repeat." Then even novice level learners will be able to practice using the target language instead of reverting back to English.
- *Develop a timeline for the year on the bulletin board.* It should show learners where they are heading at a particular level and let them mark their progress as they go. Teachers can draw lines from the timeline to samples of student work along the way. Be careful not to show a student's name along with a grade if you post student samples, because student grades are always private information.

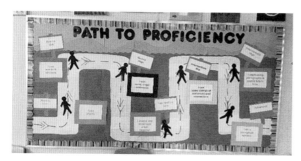

Example "Pathway to Proficiency" board: The signs along the path include benchmark proficiency statements from the NCSSFL-ACTFL Can-Do Statements.

- *Create a "Pathway to Proficiency" board that shows the proficiency levels and includes steps along the way.* You might include student work that exemplifies the proficiency sublevels, as well as *Can-Do Proficiency Benchmark Statements.*
- *Create a collage of pictures from countries where the target language is spoken.* Superior pictures can be found on large wall calendars: take the calendar apart, cut out the pictures, laminate them, and staple them onto your bulletin board. (Note: Teachers must heed copyright laws when using copyrighted materials.)

Organizing for Efficiency

At the end of your first year of teaching, you'll probably say that next year you need to be better organized. You may ask veteran colleagues for tips. Even long-time teachers admit this is an area in which they are still discovering new "tricks of the trade." All teachers seem to agree that paperwork is a major hassle. Here are some tips for getting and staying organized:

- *Have a place set up (on a cart or in the classroom) for "incoming" and "outgoing" papers.* This can be in the form of file folders by class period positioned in file holders, labeled baskets, accordion folders, "in" and "out" boxes, whatever you prefer.
- *Have a similar set-up for handouts to students.* Always keep a few extra handouts in each file so you can access them easily when students have been absent or misplace their copy. Keep appropriate handouts in the easily accessible file for the duration of the unit.

Example of an organization system: A file box for each class includes a clipboard with roster, a folder per student, and each class has its own color folders.

- *Post handouts to a learning management system, your website, or an area where students can access resources without having to ask you.* This puts the responsibility on them to secure their own materials. Parents who have access to these sites can also see what has been handed out and stay up-to-date with the instruction.
- *Post a calendar of special events, assessments, and project due dates in the class or on a mobile cart, and ask students to record the dates in a calendar.* If you have access to a learning management system, also keep the information posted online so students and parents can stay aware.
- *Have a folder for make-up quizzes or tests.* On the day of the assessment, write the name of any student who is absent on a copy of the quiz or test you distributed, date it, and put it in the folder. That way, you'll be able to locate the quiz quickly when the student comes in after school to make it up. This will also serve to remind you if the student fails to come in and make up the quiz in a timely manner.
- *Maintain a calendar to remember scheduled conferences, parent requests for a progress report, faculty meetings, due dates for interims, and everything else you are responsible for.*
- *Keep a parent contact log.* This might be a notebook or an electronic document. Each time you call, email, or receive contact from a parent, record this in the contact log. Include a brief note about the subject and, if applicable, the response. This will help you with record-keeping for parent conferences and school meetings and will give you needed documentation when an administrator requests it.

Routines help keep you organized. If you always do certain things on certain days, it's easier to remember—for example, tutor on Mondays and Wednesdays, attend meetings on Tuesdays, offer make-up assessments on Thursdays. Leave Friday afternoons for planning the next week.

Opportunities for Communication with Parents and Guardians

Back-to-School Night

This will be your first formal meeting with parents and guardians. It's an important night for you. The impression you make on the parents or guardians of your students at this event will set the tone for the year. Since middle school and high school learners can have as many as six to seven teachers, parents are usually given a schedule for their visit to each class, with travel time allowed in between. This allows them only about 10 minutes in each class, not counting time for parents or guardians who get lost and arrive late. So this time must be well organized to maximize every minute with your audience. Be sure to have the following prepared:

- Letter with basic information about the class
- Your talking points for the 10 minutes
- Contact information, so parents or guardians can contact you with any questions they may have that cannot be addressed that evening.
- A note that this evening is not a time to discuss issues for specific students, but also information on how they may set up parent-teacher conferences with you to discuss their child's needs in a private setting.

Pay special attention to the way you dress for this occasion. Professional attire is critical to assure parents that you take your job very seriously. Your appearance speaks louder than words. If a professional looks sloppy, most people fear that the service they receive will be sub-par. This is especially important if you are right out of college and only four or five years older than your students.

Before the parents and guardians arrive, set up your classroom to look inviting and make sure all of the equipment you will use in your presentation is in proper working order. Use the tips below to keep your meeting on schedule:

- Place a sign-in sheet outside the door for parents and guardians to write their names and their child's name,

or a laptop set up with an online tool such as a Google form to collect this information from them.
- Place any helpful information on the board or screen so it is easily accessible to parents and guardians when they visit the room.
- Show a portion of a student-created video on a TV monitor or projection screen as parents and guardians enter the room. This allows them to hear a bit of the language you will teach and to experience just how different language classes are today.
- Collect needed information from parents and guardians, either through an online tool such as a Google form or with index cards they can complete while visiting the class. On these forms or cards they can ask questions about something you did not address or make a note about something they feel you should know about their children. (This facilitates communication with parents and guardians while preventing specific student-related questions from bogging down your program).
- Distribute a Back-to-School Night brochure or handout containing all of your talking points so parents and guardians do not feel they have to take detailed notes during your presentation. Be sure to also post this information on your website for them to refer to later, or for those who could not attend your presentation.

During your presentation, be sure to address the following:

Objectives. Parents and guardians should know what their children will be able to do by the end of the year at that level. Use Can-Do Statements, and alert parents and guardians to focus on how learners demonstrate the goal, and how valuable it is to them. Demonstrate a two-minute immersion in the language so the parents and guardians understand why and how your teaching strategies work. Once they experience how they were able to do something in the target language, they will be able to support you in helping learners understand the need for immersion in the language.

Resources. Show parents and guardians the types of resources that will be used. If learners need access to particular apps or sites, be sure to explain this.

Classroom rules and teacher expectations. Briefly explain your grading policy and how parents and guardians can help monitor their children's progress. Remind them of the policies that were sent home at the beginning of the year, and encourage them to contact you if they have questions.

Progress reports. Tell parents and guardians how they can access students' grades, and when they can expect to be notified of their children's progress—for example, if a student (1) drops one letter grade, (2) fails a major test, (3) does not turn in three assignments, or (4) fails to have an interim report signed.

Study strategies. Give parents and guardians tips on effective study strategies so they can assist in ensuring their child's progress.

And since these talking points will probably take up most of your time, be sure you remind parents how they can contact you whenever they have additional questions.

Your Letter to Parents and Guardians

Prepare a letter with basic information to give to parents and guardians at the back-to-school event or to send home on the first day of class. This document makes an important impression, just like meeting parents for the first time in person. Parents and guardians want to know from the start the answers to important questions, such as:

- Is this teacher positive and enthusiastic about teaching?
- Will s/he be fair to my child?
- What are the expectations for my child?
- How can my child be successful in this class?
- How can I help my child be successful?

In your letter, answer all these questions in your own words. Keep it brief, but cogent. This information for parents can be shared in multiple ways. You can distribute hard copies of letters and the letter should be posted on your website as well.

Before printing or posting your letter, ask a member of your department to proofread it for you. You might want to ask an administrator to review the letter. It's important to make a good first impression with a well-written, error-free letter. You do not want parents or guardians to see any spelling, grammar or punctuation errors, because they will think: (1) you do not know how to write English correctly, (2) you will be careless in grading their children's work, and (3) you do not take pride in your work.

> ❓ In communication with parents, administrators, and other stakeholders, correct grammar, spelling and punctuation are important. The way in which you communicate reflects upon your level of professionalism. Errors and a casual style that might be acceptable when texting with friends are unacceptable when communicating professionally.

In your letter, give parents contact information, including a phone number, an email address, and a website address. For your protection and privacy, it is best not to share your personal cell phone number with parents and guardians or students. Provide the school phone number, or consider using tools such as Remind 101 or a Google Voice number to facilitate communication with parents and guardians without giving personal information. An open line of communication gives them a secure feeling that you share the mission of helping their child succeed. Make your letter as inviting and helpful as possible, and send it home or have it posted online the first day of school. Parents and guardians especially look forward to reading the information students bring home after their first day of school. Ask them to sign and return the bottom part of the letter indicating how they prefer to be contacted during the school year.

Note: Imagine how you would feel if you received five or six different messages with different instructions for each hour of the day. Our learners and their parents or guardians likely feel the same way. A suggestion here would be to use email as an alternative. It's possible to ask the students to request that their parents or guardians send you an email indicating how they would prefer to be contacted. If a teacher does not hear from a parent, the teacher knows that a follow up is necessary to initiate contact. Teachers can make this the assignment, keep track of the emails, create class lists, and send the initial letter electronically. Many schools restrict paper and encourage email. Many parents and guardians prefer this type of contact, since letters do not arrive home. It is important to know if all parents and guardians have access to email or the Internet. If not, you can tell those without access that you will be sending home information on certain days.

Your letter to parents and guardians should also include relevant information about the course and your policies. They want to know the content that will be addressed, the skills learners will gain, the grading policies, and your means of contact. (Examples of parent letters with various grading systems are included at the end of this chapter.)

> ✓ What are your school's grading, attendance, and discipline policies? Be sure that your information to parents and guardians aligns with these policies.

The following items should be included in your letter:
- Course title and course code (if applicable)
- Credit upon completion (if applicable)
- Classroom number (if applicable)
- Information on how to get in touch with you
- Instructional resources to be used in the class
- Materials needed
- Course description, with goals and objectives
- Content to be addressed by quarter, semester, or year. This may include short explanations of the *World-Readiness Standards* and/or the *NCSSFL-ACTFL Can-Do Statements*. (See Appendices B and C)
- Teacher website address and/or information on how to access online resources
- Grading system and policies
- How parents and guardians can keep up with their child's progress
- Policies and/or rules regarding lateness, attendance, cheating, grading, class participation, missed assignments (Be sure these are aligned with school or district policies)
- Available sources of support
- Information regarding access to a course website or online materials

Parent-Teacher Conferences

Parent conferences are much more productive if you have made contact with the parent or guardian in a positive manner prior to the meeting. Starting the year on a positive note usually develops an atmosphere of collaboration with the parent.

It is always a good strategy to contact the parent or guardian of a student who may need extra help to mention the good things s/he is doing in class and perhaps suggest one additional strategy that may make things even better. Always use the "compliment sandwich" approach. Start with saying something positive, then express your concern, then follow the concern with something else positive. Don't shy away from the concern in this approach. Be clear but respectful in expressing the concern. If you feel another phone call or email is necessary, in the second contact you should also offer helpful suggestions. You could also mention to the parent or guardian a particular strategy that may have worked in the past or your observation that the student was much better prepared because of the extra effort exerted on the homework assignment.

If a parent or guardian requests a conference because the student is not showing progress or his/her work is actually declining, your tone should be helpful, such as "Let's brainstorm some ways to help Jane succeed," rather than placing blame on anyone.

On the day of the conference, arrive at the meeting on time and fully prepared to discuss the student's performance. Come prepared with the following:
- *A list of the student's grades and a current average for the grading period as of the day of the conference.* Be sure you have graded any work the student has made up or completed, even if the work from the other students has not yet been graded.
- *Samples of the student's work.* If you want the parent or guardian to understand that the student's work is always incomplete, then it is much more effective to show a sample of an actual incomplete assignment or examples of the student's work that did not meet expectations. Be prepared to explain the expectation and how the work did not meet it. This will show concrete evidence for a poor grade and will help keep the conversation about the student's performance objective.
- *Attendance record.* If attendance (or late arrivals to class) is the problem, have all of the student's absent dates listed. Any make-up work that hasn't been turned in should also be listed so the parent or guardian is fully informed and can help get the student "back on track."
- *A recommended plan of action.* A parent or guardian is taking the time to come in and talk to you because s/he is concerned about the child's progress and wants to leave with a sense of hope that things will turn around. If you can work with him/her on strategies that both you and s/he can follow and a plan for the student to take responsibility for his/her learning, the parent or guardian probably will leave with the feeling that the

school is just as concerned about this student as s/he is. The plan should include:

- How you will communicate with the parent or guardian.
- A date for the next conference.
- Measurable goals and objectives for the student.
- Strategies to help the student meet these goals.
- An evaluation design—how you and the parent or guardian will know these goals have been met.
- *Recommended resources.* Some parents or guardians are at a complete loss as to how to help their children. So be prepared to give them information on local tutors, digital tools such as apps and websites, outside resources such as books, CDs, movies, or games in the target language, and peer tutoring information.

It would also be helpful for you to:

- *Include the student in the conference.* Students can share the learning objectives from the Can-Do Statements and explain their evidence of the Can-Dos. This focuses the discussion on specific learning goals, what the student does or does not understand, and a plan for support. Additionally, both the student and the parent or guardian must hear the same message from you, and vice versa. It also helps establish a "team" approach to helping the student improve.
- *Consider having an administrator present.* If you are concerned about the potential challenges of a particular conference, you may want to ask a counselor or administrator to be present at the parent-teacher meeting. It can be helpful to have a third party in the discussion, especially if you think the discussion could become contentious.

Communicating Beyond the Classroom

You must be able to communicate with parents and the community at large about the world language program and perhaps other issues at your school. (Examples of invitation and thank-you letters are provided at the end of the chapter.) It would be great if such communication were always supportive, but at times you may be confronted with negative comments or questions about your school or program. If that happens, don't panic. Stay calm. Then consider carefully how you will respond. First, be professional in your response. Here are a few tips to help you deal with such situations:

To whom will you respond?

- Shape your response with awareness and consideration of the person or group you are addressing.

How much does the constituency know about the subject?

- Did the person or persons get information from a student, neighbor, or friend?
- Do you and they have the facts, or is the knowledge based on hearsay?

What was the purpose of the original communication?

- Be sure you understand the question.
- Are legal ramifications likely?
- What is the context of this communication? Are there undercurrents in it? Is this an attempt to discredit you or a staff member?
- Be aware of the respondent's slant or point of view. Listen or look for phrases such as "in my opinion," or vague words such as "people," "peers," or "groups."
- What seems to be the key source of the concern or hostility?
- Always respond to your correspondent with a sincere, straightforward, tactful answer.

Crafting a response

- Is your response an acknowledgment?
- Are you providing information, explanation, and/or clarification?
- Are you responding to defend department policy?
- Do not write or respond verbally while you are angry.
- Put the message aside, take time to think about your response, and leave your personal emotion out of the response. Aim to defuse the situation.
- Never use sarcasm.
- Do not state facts you cannot prove.
- Use objectivity and facts; avoid opinions.

Style and tone

- Use a clear and concise writing style, imparting clear ideas in a few words.
- Eliminate extra words or superfluous information.
- Impart ideas briefly and straightforwardly.

- How can the data be presented fairly? Find neutral ground.
- Be sure to address the heart of the matter. If you're not sure about it, ask colleagues and supervisors for assistance.
- Always treat the correspondent with integrity and respect.
- Remember that in email or letters the recipient cannot read your tone. Avoid language that could be interpreted negatively.

Closing remarks

- Be firm but professional.
- Close on a positive note, thanking the writer for expressing his/her viewpoint.
- Display a true sense of concern and an offer to help.

Connections with Learners

It's important to find out what makes your students tick. In the first month of school you can ask learners many questions to get them back into speaking the target language. As a warm-up exercise, ask questions from which you can learn what students like to do in their free time, their favorite movies, books, sports, pets, food, etc. Some educators ask students to create collages describing all of this information about them, with their photos in the middle of the collages. This usually opens up communication in a creative way, lets students know a little more about each other, and gives you valuable insight into each learner's world. If you expect students to really communicate with one another, they need to get to know each other and learn to care about one another. One teacher using this technique wrote each student's likes and dislikes on a seating chart. In classroom sessions, her students couldn't believe how much their teacher remembered about each of them throughout the year!

A word of caution: Be careful about the ways in which you build connections with your students. Some may want to "friend" you on Instagram, Snapchat, or other social media outlets. While this is a way to connect with students, it can also be an easy way to get in trouble. Most of all, be sure you are aware of school or district policies regarding social media and teacher-student contacts. A policy may ban or restrict such interactions.

You should not extend or accept friend requests to or from students with your personal social media accounts. Remember, you must be the professional adult, not your students' "friend," even when trying to build relationships with them. However, if your school or district's policies allow, you could have a professional social media account for sharing information with students and/or parents and guardians, displaying student work, and connecting with students in a limited way. When posting to such an account, separate the personal from the professional.

> ❓ Building positive rapport with students is a key to management. How will you work to build rapport in positive and professional ways?

Student Recognition

Most students love attention, negative or positive. Never forget the power of positive attention and the results that can come from it. Every classroom has students who go through the system with little or no recognition year after year. They do not have the stellar grades, athletic talent, or popularity of students who are often in the limelight, nor do they have other student's discipline issues. They do what they are told and ask for very little in return. Yet they watch the same students win awards and receive recognition time and time again.

Don't take the quiet disposition of these learners for granted, thinking they are doing what is expected of them and forgetting to reward them for their accomplishments as good classroom citizens. The real reward of teaching is to give such students positive attention and watch them blossom. Recognize students who:

- Bring their books to class every day for a grading period.
- Cooperate in group work activities every time.
- Come to class on time every day.
- Have perfect attendance for a grading period.
- Share materials with classmates who forget to bring something.
- Exhibit the most effort on their work.
- Show the most improvement.
- Actively participate in class several days in a row.
- Volunteer to help classmates.
- Help decorate a bulletin board.
- Follow all class rules.

Ideas for recognition:

- A pencil imprinted with a slogan in the target language.
- An appreciation certificate.
- Recognition stickers (believe it or not, even high-schoolers like stickers).
- Recognition beads (to add on a belt or necklace).
- Fake coins that can be collected and "cashed in" for rewards at the end of a grading period.
- Posting the student's name on a recognition board (e.g., "Student of the Week").

An especially powerful way to reward a learner is to call attention in class to his/her activity beyond the language classroom. For example, give students credit for performance in sporting events, plays, choral concerts, debate team presentations, or artwork in an exhibit. If a student isn't excelling in your language course, s/he may excel in another area. It means so much for students to know that their teacher came to see their accomplishments in another discipline or extracurricular activity. Often when students feel their teacher cares about them in this way, they will put forth a little more effort so as not to disappoint the teacher. Positive attention wins respect, helps to develop positive rapport, and can turn a learner around. It is always a treat when a graduate comes back to visit and tells the teacher that a particular act on the teacher's part meant so much.

Letters and Endorsements for Students

You will be asked at various times to time to write letters of recommendation for students. You may also need to write thank you letters, invitations to school events, commendations, and responses to parent concerns. Over the years many teachers develop a file of letters they can use as templates for new drafts of letters and documents.

As a new teacher, writing letters may seem daunting at first. How should you begin your letter? How much should you write? What should be included? This handbook includes letter templates for many situations, designed to jump-start the process for you. Modifications will definitely be needed, but the templates will save you considerable time. As a rule of thumb, keep letters short. Get to your point early on. Keep letters to one page if at all possible. (An example letter is at the end of this chapter.)

Here are some tips about formatting letters to make them clear and precise:

- Include an opening statement and orientation, in which you:
  - Introduce yourself.
  - State the reason for the letter.
  - Acknowledge a previous letter.
  - Provide specific information.
- In the body of the letter, you should:
  - Explain background details. In the case of an invitation to an event, describe the sponsoring organization and the significance of the event.
  - In a recommendation, cite specific examples to back up your positive remarks.
  - In response to a parental concern, clarify what action has been taken and any further steps proposed.
- Be sure your letter:
  - Displays empathy with your correspondent, so s/he will feel that you have taken his/her feelings into account.
  - Backs up what you have said with details and other references.
  - Asks the person to take specific action.
  - Thanks the person in advance for being willing to comply with your request, and for his/her time and effort in the endeavor.

Remember, letters should be saved. Create a file for them. You can use them for proof of participation, to answer routine questions, or to prepare responses (with a few modifications) to requests you receive from individuals and organizations. Of course, always proofread your letters carefully, and don't write anything you can't back up with documentation.

Colleagues: A Valuable Resource

Before school starts, get to know colleagues, especially experienced teachers, who teach courses identical or similar to yours. They will usually be happy to share information you may find crucial for planning and pacing your first month on the job. Ask questions that will help you with immediate issues. Avoid being drawn into long conversations about issues that do not concern you or your course. To stay on topic, write down your questions in advance. In those questions, ask for specific information you'll need to create your syllabus, your letter to parents, and your lessons for the first weeks. Some suggested questions:

- Are there school or district policies on grading, class participation, homework, cheating, classroom rules I need to know about so I can develop my policies accordingly?
- Did you integrate last year's material (Level 2 class or above) throughout your lessons this year?
- What is your grading system?
- What types of assessments do you use?
- What materials do you use to supplement the textbook?
- Where can I find a copy of the curriculum guide?
- How much material are you able to address in the first grading period?
- Does the department use common assessments, performance assessments, or departmental exams? Could I get copies before I start planning?
- Do we have common planning time?

- Does the department share materials? Are they in a central location?
- What kind of technology and devices can we access?
- What can students access?
- Is there a language lab?
- How do we sign up for shared resources or tools, such as a laptop cart?

> **?** Does your school assign mentors to new teachers? This person can be an invaluable resource. If not, consider requesting one from the administration.

Am I ready?

☑ step 1
☐ step 2

☐ I have established a language-rich and culture-rich **classroom environment** in which learners will feel welcomed and enthusiastic about learning the target language.

☐ I have developed a system for **calling students by name**, even on the first day.

☐ I have a well-developed plan for **classroom management**.

☐ My expectations are clear.

☐ I have every minute accounted for in my lesson plan so there is no down-time. My lessons are engaging.

☐ My students understand why they are doing a particular activity.

☐ My lesson objectives are clearly stated and posted where students can see them. I avoid the use of "busy work."

☐ I have developed classroom rules that are positive, simple, and concise.

☐ I use the same classroom rules consistently. Students see me as a figure of authority.

☐ I follow through with consequences for students. I have the respect of my students.

☐ I follow my own rules.

☐ I have developed a **seating arrangement** that will encourage communication and collaboration.

☐ I am **organized**:

  ☐ I have a system in place for students to turn in work electronically and/or in hard copy.

  ☐ I have a plan in place for storing handouts and assignments so students can access them easily when they have been absent.

  ☐ I have a calendar (electronic or hard copy) posted for special events, assessments, and projects.

  ☐ I have a calendar (electronic or hard copy) to record conferences, meetings, parent/guardian requests, etc.

  ☐ I have a contact log prepared (electronic or hard copy).

  ☐ I have organized my website and/or learning management system course so parents, guardians, and students can access needed information and resources.

☐ I have developed a **Back-to-School** handout for parents, guardians, and students:

  ☐ Classroom number

  ☐ Information on how to get in touch with me

  ☐ Instructional resources to be used in class

  ☐ Materials needed

  ☐ Course description, with goals and objectives

  ☐ Content to be addressed by quarter, semester, or year (this may include short explanations of the *World-Readiness Standards* and/or the *NCSSFL-ACTFL Can-Do Statements*)

  ☐ Teacher website address and/or information about how to access online resources

  ☐ Grading system/policies

  ☐ How parents and guardians can keep up with their child's progress

  ☐ Policies and/or rules regarding lateness, attendance, cheating, grading, class participation, and missed assignments (aligned with school policies)

  ☐ Available sources of support

  ☐ Information on access to a course website or online materials

☐ I have a plan to **communicate** regularly with parents and guardians.

☐ I am prepared for **parent-teacher conferences** and know to bring with me the following:
- ☐ A list of the student's grades and a current average for the grading period as of the day of the conference
- ☐ Samples of the student's work
- ☐ Attendance record
- ☐ Parent/guardian contact log
- ☐ A recommended Plan of Action
- ☐ My calendar in case the parents or guardians want a follow-up conference

☐ I plan to **recognize students** for not only achievement, but also effort and success outside of the classroom.

☐ I have selected clothing that is appropriate for my **professional** position.

☐ I have a mentor or know **colleagues** of whom I can ask questions.

Reflection

What aspects of this chapter worked well?

What would I change for next year?

How would I change it?

What additional resources do I need to gather for next year?

Template K | Classroom Rules

K-8

Classroom Rules and Procedures

Sensational Sensei
Japanese 1

1

Respect your fellow classmates, your teacher,
and the classroom contents at all times.

2

Come prepared to learn by bringing your materials.

3

Food and gum interfere with oral communication.
Please leave these items in your backpack or locker.

4

Ask for clarification when you are confused.
There are no dumb questions.

5

Only use cell phones when directed to by the teacher.

Template L | Student Responsibility

High School

What Is Student Responsibility?

1. The state, quality, or fact of being responsible.
2. Something for which one is responsible; a duty, obligation, or burden
   (see *http://dictionary.reference.com/search?q=responsibility*).

What Is Cheating?

I. The following constitutes cheating in my class:
   a. Using Google Translate or other automatic translation tools.
   b. Giving or receiving information on assessments.
   c. Using any type of unapproved aide during formal or informal assessments (electronic devices, cheat sheets, etc.).
   d. Copying from another student's tests, quizzes, homework, and projects.
   e. Discussing content material with students who have not yet taken an assessment.
   f. Parental help beyond that of assistance.
   g. Plagiarism: copying the essential character of another's work, whether visual or written, and submitting it as your own.

II. Consequences for your actions:
   a. I will have a conversation with your parent or guardian.
   b. Your administrator and guidance counselor will be notified.
   c. You will not receive credit for the work that was compromised.
   d. You will have to redo the work by completing an alternate assignment.
   e. You will have to work hard to earn my trust again.

I will gladly write letters of recommendation for any student who has resisted the temptation to cheat.

Template M | Class Participation

Class Participation Self-Assessment

Class participation is a key component in practicing your communicative skills, which are essential in language proficiency. Participation involves more than just raising your hand. Students must be attentive, participate in partner activities, speak the target language formally and informally, and come to class prepared. If your teacher agrees that you exceed expectations in these areas, you will be able to drop your lowest quiz grade at the end of the quarter. These weekly self-assessments will keep you focused on your progress.

Name: _____ Period: _____ Date: _____

Place a check in the box indicating your participation in these activities over the past week:

1 = occasionally, 2 = half the time, 3 = most of the time, 4 = always

Activity	1	2	3	4
I brought my materials to class.				
I paid attention in class and conversed only when asked to do so.				
I raised my hand to answer questions.				
I participated in partner activities.				
I participated in other activities.				
I spoke the target language with the teacher.				
I spoke the target language with peers.				
I came to class with my homework completed and was able to participate when my teacher went over the assignment.				
Student's Self-Assessment Total Score: _____ /32				
Teacher's Validation Score: _____ /32				

Template N | Letter to Parents
(Modern Language, Standards-Based Grading System)

High
School

(date)

Dear Parents and Guardians,

Welcome to *la Classe de Français*! I have some exciting news to share with you regarding French class this year, and I am asking for your support in this venture. The overall goal of my class is to help students prepare to use French in real-world ways. To help students achieve this goal more readily, I will use a standards-based grading system. This is slightly different than the traditional grading system many teachers use. It moves away from separate grade categories for quizzes, tests, classwork, and participation and instead focuses on assessing the three modes of communication: **Interpretive** (reading, listening), **Interpersonal** (speaking in conversations), and **Presentational** (speaking, writing to an audience).

This gradebook splits between learning practice (10%) and performance-based tasks (90%) that show what students can do with language in each mode in the real world. Instruction is aligned to the North Carolina World Language Essential Standards, which are built on the three modes of communication. Students will have a great deal of learning practice that will help them prepare for multiple opportunities each quarter to be assessed in each of the three categories.

Proficiency-Based Gradebook Categories

Category	%	Description
Learning Practice	10%	Grades in this category reflect the preparation work you will do to use the language in real-world ways. Homework, participation, in-class work, and checks on specific language elements (vocabulary, structures) are in this category.
Interpersonal *(Speaking)*	30%	The interpersonal mode of communication measures how well you speak the language in interaction with others and is the mode that prepares you to use the language in spontaneous conversations. You speak or write to exchange information in natural ways, and you do not have a chance to script or memorize conversations or dialogues.
Interpretive *(Reading and Listening)*	30%	The interpretive mode of communication measures how well you understand spoken or written authentic materials. There is no opportunity to interact with others, so you must be able to understand the spoken, viewed or written text on your own.
Presentational *(Speaking or Writing)*	30%	The presentational mode of communication allows you to think about what you will say or write. When writing, you may have time to draft and revise before producing a final product. When speaking, you may be able to rehearse and/or record multiple times until you are satisfied with the final product.

After consulting with experts in the field and reading lots of research, I believe that one important step to helping students focus on their learning is to make the gradebook reflective of their true performance in the classroom. Students will receive meaningful feedback on assignments that will help communicate how well they are doing on reaching the targeted level of proficiency. Students will receive ample opportunities to show how they are working toward proficiency in each of the three modes. As always, you will be able to track your child's progress in Powerschool.

This may be a shift for students and for you in how they earn grades. I truly believe that this shift will be a positive one that magnifies learning for all involved.

We will use many authentic resources and materials in this class. Students need a composition notebook and will be asked to use sites/apps such as Google classroom and Flipgrid.

I appreciate your support! If you have any questions, please do not hesitate to call/email me. Thank you again for your support!

Sincerely,

Madame Merveilleuse
(phone and email info)

Template O | Letter to Parents
(Classical Language, Traditional Grading)

High School

Mountain View High School   *Home of the Mountain View Tigers*

5345 Tiger Trail   [date]
Pleasant Town, USA 12345

Dear Parents and Guardians,

I am pleased to have your son/daughter in my **Latin 1** class. I plan to make his/her year of studying a language an exciting and memorable experience.

World language study is essential today, not only to meet the requirements of higher education institutions, but also because of the expanding global economy and the ever-increasing job opportunities domestically that require one or more languages other than English. Students will benefit from learning **Latin,** no matter what academic or career path they pursue.

The relationship of English to **Latin** is emphasized in vocabulary building, word derivation, and meanings of prefixes and suffixes. Language structures and syntax are developed through the study of literary passages. At the beginning of each grading period, I will send home objectives for the nine weeks. If you have any questions about the program, please feel free to contact me at [phone number] or email me at faye.fantastic@mountainview.edu.

To strengthen your child's organizational skills, I will issue each student a Mountain View Planner, in which s/he is to write assignments and quizzes/tests/projects at the beginning of each week. Please check your child's planner regularly to be informed of the daily activities. Homework assignments will be kept to an average of 15-20 minutes per day. Students and parents can access grades at any time through the online portal. Progress reports are issued halfway through each quarter.

Student grades are based on a point system. Each grade the student receives on a quiz, test, oral presentation, project, class participation, etc., will be worth a certain number of points based on a 100-point scale. Quarter and final grades will be based on the school district's grading scale, which is:

94 - 100	A
87 - 93	B
80 - 86	C
70 - 79	D
Below 70	F

At the end of the grading period, the total number of points earned will be divided by the total number of points possible. Each grade has the following weight for the quarter grade:

Tests	30%
Quizzes	20%
Projects	25%
Homework	15%
Class Participation	10%

Students do not receive grades lower than 50% unless the student refuses to complete the assignment or is caught cheating. The final grade for the year is an average of the four quarter grades and the final exam.

We will use the textbook, along with other authentic resources and materials in this class. Students will require a composition notebook and will be asked to use sites/apps such as Google classroom and Flipgrid.

I expect this to be an exciting and fulfilling year in your child's language experience. I look forward to meeting you at Back-to-School Night on [date].

Sincerely,

Faye Fantastic

Template P | Information for Parents
(Modern Language, Traditional Grading)

High School

Syllabus for Arabic 1

Contact Info: teacher@email.com; [Google voice number here]

Materials needed: Students will need to bring to class a three-ring binder with pockets and dividers, paper, pencil/pen

Course Description: Students develop the ability to communicate about themselves and their immediate environment using simple sentences containing basic language structures. Students will develop intercultural skills as well as language skills in the three modes of communication: Interpretive, Interpersonal, and Presentational. Students will explore and study the themes of Personal and Family Life, School Life, Social Life, and Community Life.

Goals: This course's primary goals are to:
- **Communicate in Arabic:** Students function in a variety of practical settings using interpretive, interpersonal and presentational communication in culturally appropriate ways.
- **Understand other cultures:** Students will investigate, explain, and reflect on cultural products, practices and perspectives.
- **Connect with other disciplines and acquire information:** Students connect information about the language and cultures they are learning with concepts studied in other content areas.
- **Make comparisons:** Through study of language and culture, students recognize, compare and contrast language concepts as well as cultural perspectives, practices and products.
- **Participate in the global community:** Students use the target language to communicate with speakers of that language, both at home and around the world, to improve their own communication skills and to enhance their view of themselves as citizens of the world.

Content to be addressed in the first quarter:
Theme: Personal and Family Life Greeting and Introductions Physical Descriptions Family Members

Assessments: Students will be assessed formally and informally through tests, quizzes, projects, homework assignments, and class participation. These assessments will measure language learning in the three modes of communication: Interpretive (reading/listening), Interpersonal (conversation), and Presentational (speaking/writing). The district has developed and uses performance assessments as tools to measure language progress. These are conducted routinely throughout the year and rated using rubrics developed by language teachers. The end-of-year assessment includes performance in the three modes of communication.

Tardies: After two tardies, I will notify parents and assign the student an after-school detention, in accord with school policy.

Homework: It is necessary to practice Arabic daily to build a solid foundation for future lessons. To accomplish this objective, homework will be assigned at the end of each class period. I will post the weekly assignments, quizzes, and tests on the board in front of the class and on my website. It will be your responsibility to record the assignments in your assignment book. If you have been absent, you will know the assignment that has been missed.

Class Participation: Class participation in the target language is a key component in practicing your communicative skills, which are essential in language proficiency. Participation involves more than just raising your hand. Students must be attentive, participate in partner activities, speak the target language formally and informally, and come to class prepared. If your teacher agrees that you exceed expectations in this area, you will be able to drop your lowest quiz grade at the end of the quarter. These self-assessments will be conducted weekly to keep you focused on your progress.

Grading: Student grades are based on a point system. Each grade the student receives (quiz, test, oral presentation, project, class participation, etc.) will be worth a certain number of points as determined by the teacher. At the end of the grading period, the total number of points earned will be divided by the total number of points possible. Each grade has the following weight for the quarter grade:

Tests	30%
Quizzes	20%
Projects	25%
Homework	15%
Class Participation	10%

Extra help: I am available after school on Mondays and Wednesdays in my room. Please schedule to stay after school with me if you feel you need extra help. It is better to ask for extra help as soon as there is confusion. We also have honor society students willing to tutor students, if you or they prefer a peer tutor.

Template Q | Recommendation for Student

High
School

[date]

To whom it may concern:

It is with great pleasure that I am able to recommend Alison Angel. Alison is a dynamic, intelligent high school junior at Mountain View High School. Last year I had the pleasure of having this extremely gifted student in my Spanish 3 class, and this year she is continuing with the AP Spanish Language course. Alison enjoys learning and taking on challenges. She represents the best of what an American high school student can be: motivated enough to set high standards and hard-working enough to achieve those lofty goals.

In Spanish—and I am sure it is the same in her other classes—she has never had an unexcused lateness or absence. Rather, she arrives first to class and is always prepared to learn. Dedicated to her studies, Alison thrives in a challenging and scholarly environment. She never turns in a late or incomplete assignment. In fact, Alison expects the most from herself and maintains a 4.0 in Spanish. Although Alison carries the highest grade of any student I teach, she readily completes any extra credit assignment I assign. She simply wants to perfect her language skills on a continual basis. She has always had the curiosity and the drive to search for a challenging opportunity to enrich her proficiency in a subject area. I highly recommend Alison for acceptance at your institution.

Alison consistently selects and succeeds at Mountain View's toughest courses. She is able to balance her academics with her extracurricular activities. She is in the Spanish Honor Society and the National Honor Society and has won numerous academic honors.

Alison's hard work and dedication are true character traits, which separate her from many other students I have taught. When any student in the class does not understand a concept, she does not hesitate to help that student. She is a silent leader and is admired by her peers. Through her persistence, she has developed into an excellent Spanish student striving for more.

Alison Angel is quite simply a wonderfully talented young woman with a strong intellect and exemplary personal values, who will be a tremendous asset wherever she goes. She is a role model for peers and adults alike and is accorded a great deal of respect by all of those who come in contact with her. It is with the highest degree of confidence and enthusiasm that I recommend her.

Sincerely,

Jeff Baxter
Spanish Instructor

Template R | Thank You Letter

[date]

Mr. John Doe
1000 Any Street
Any Town, State, Zip

Dear Mr. Doe,

I want to thank you so much for providing bagels for our teachers at our World Language staff development program on [date]. Refreshments are such an important part of any conference or in-service. Once the teachers had enjoyed the breakfast, they were invigorated and ready to begin the morning session. Thank you so much for thinking of us, as usual.

Let me also thank you, on behalf of the teachers, for the excellent support we always received from the PTA.

As the Spanish teacher at Mountain View High School, I look forward to working with you throughout the school year.

Sincerely,

Sally McBride
World Language Coordinator

Template S

Invitation to School Event

High School

Dear Parents:

The World Language Department will host the second annual International Night on [date] at [time]. The students and faculty wish to extend an invitation to you and your family to join in the festivities. Enclosed you will find a pass to admit you and your family to the concert following the open house, as well as a schedule so that you can plan your evening.

We know you will enjoy the event. The students would also welcome your attendance at the presentation of awards shortly after the concert to acknowledge the hard work and achievements this event represents.

We look forward to seeing you on [date]. If you have any questions or need additional information, please call _____ at _____.

Sincerely,

[Teacher]
[School]

Chapter 4 | How Do I Handle Challenging Moments?

Everyone has moments when things do not seem to work out as planned. Teachers are no exception. You can't prevent these moments from occurring, but you can do some things now that will prepare you to deal with surprises when they occur.

The most important thing to remember is to be flexible! This chapter will give you some tried-and-true ideas about preparing for the unexpected. All teachers need backup plans in their toolboxes. Experienced teachers usually do, because they have faced wacky situations in their careers at one time or another. As a first-year teacher, you are most in jeopardy when mishaps occur unexpectedly to derail your classroom plan. Being caught off-guard slows down the problem-solving process, adding to your duress.

This chapter will give you examples of what kinds of emergencies could happen in your classroom and time-tested solutions that can at least limit your grief when the unexpected occurs.

The Traveling Teacher

What if you find yourself traveling from room to room, with no permanent base? Before school begins, work out a system with the teachers who also use the classroom. Ask if you can have a bookcase, a table, a portion of a bulletin board or wall space, a drawer of a file cabinet, a shelf of a wardrobe, drop boxes, and/or a file folder stand.

You may want to locate or request a mobile cart, which can become your mobile desk. It will need a place to store handouts, resources, whiteboard markers, extra paper and pencils, and other materials. Some traveling teachers post their classroom rules on their carts, and students regard the cart as a place to deposit homework, pick up worksheets, and even get a pencil if they have forgotten to bring one. If you have a cart, you'll always have your materials with you. The key to being a traveling teacher—and a teacher in general—is to stay organized!

Mid-Lesson Changes

Every teacher must admit that every now and then a lesson plan bombs. You could be in the middle of what you thought was a wonderful lesson and notice that not one student is paying attention, and your students appear clueless about what you are imparting to them. What do you do? Here are your choices:

- Continue on as if nothing is going wrong. You spent hours last night writing this lesson and will deliver it.
- Change activities, but keep the focus on the same topic, and see if you can re-engage the students.
- Stop and ask learners for feedback. Check to see if:
  - They are confused about the content or objectives.
  - They understand the purpose for the lesson. (Did you take time to explain how this lesson fits into the "big picture"?)
  - They have experienced "information overload" and need time to digest the material.
  - They need more time to practice what they have learned.
  - Your expectations are too high or too low.
  - They understand where you are going with the lesson.

Usually a few questions will give you the information you need to proceed. Once you have identified the cause of the lesson malfunction, back up and regroup. Be prepared to go back and explain things again. Always have a Plan B. The following tips will help you develop one:

- Do a "brain break" activity. (See Chapter 2 for a few ideas.)
- Divide the class into groups, and assign each group a different topic to research and "teach" on the subject you wanted to cover. When learners have to teach vocabulary, a cultural point, demonstrate the use of vocabulary in a dialogue or skit, you can turn passive learning into active learning and involve students in reaching the desired goals.
- Keep a folder of pictures (hard copy or electronic) handy for use with any topic. Use art from the target culture as a source for pictures to naturally imbed culture. Use the

pictures to elicit conversation, write a dialogue, write a journal entry, create a story, or describe family members, clothing, weather, activities, etc., that involves students in your lesson. This is a good way to involve the students and give them more opportunities to actually use the concepts you are teaching.

- Ask two teams of students to reach into a hat and pull out a scenario. Each team acts out the scenario described on the card. The students vote on the best "improv," and the team with the most votes gets a certificate. After 10 or 15 minutes, you will likely find your students focused and ready for another activity.

- If you find that your expectations for this lesson were too high, shift gears and let students master smaller units before proceeding. This will also give them more confidence to tackle more challenging units later. You can revise your lesson plan and continue it in the next class, and you'll probably find students participating to a greater degree, because they now have a better grasp of the basics.

- If students seem "lost," form small groups and ask them to discuss the major concepts that have been taught. Jot them down on a piece of newsprint and ask a member of each group to report the group's thoughts and conclusions on the subject. Group discussions help students who missed some portions of the lesson to "catch up."

It's okay to be honest with learners and admit that perhaps your lesson was a bit too ambitious. Students will appreciate your sensitivity about stopping to reteach or reorganize. They are savvy. If they sense that you want to get from A to Z whether or not all of your students are keeping up with the work, they may give up and tune out. Always read your learners' body language and ask frequent questions to be constantly aware of how your lesson is going. Also be prepared to have a very successful lesson from one year off track the very next year. Students are different. So when you plan lessons, always consider the makeup of your class, and have a backup plan at all times.

Emergency Lesson Plans

Admit it: Teachers are not "superheroes," even if their deeds may entitle them to that status. You can get sick. Your car can break down on the way to work. Unanticipated events that will keep you out of your classroom can happen. So you need to plan for them.

Before the school year begins, develop a lesson plan that covers three days and is not tied to any particular unit. This may sound challenging, but it really isn't all that difficult, and it will save you from having to write lesson plans at 2:00 a.m. because you can't be at school that day. The objective is to allow students to continue to learn in the teacher's absence.

> ✅ With any plan for a substitute teacher, be sure to leave a copy of your class schedule and any pertinent information regarding routines, expectations, and how students are to submit their work.

Don't design an emergency lesson plan just to keep the students busy. Make sure it has an important instructional objective. Make your plan meaningful and easy for a substitute teacher to deliver. If you teach two or more levels, try to develop emergency lesson plans that can be used in all of your classes.

The following are suggestions for lessons that can be taught by a non-speaker of the language you teach; many language teachers will not have access to substitute teachers who speak the target language. (Emergency lesson plan examples are at the end of this chapter.)

- *Geography lesson:* Students can always benefit from a short lesson or refresher lesson on geography and map-reading in the country of the target language. Students can also use websites for a geography scavenger hunt or plan what to see and do in a particular country or city.

- *Children's book:* Students may enjoy writing a children's book in the target language, with illustrations. Even Level 1 students can write a short story with greetings, numbers, common phrases, etc. They may be impressed that they can actually produce something in the target language and read it aloud to a small group. The illustrations will add some fun to the project. If the substitute teacher can access a computer lab, or if students can access devices, they may use pictures and creative fonts to give their books a polished look.

- *Famous people project:* Have biographies of 10 or 15 well-known people from the target language country. Ask each student to select a person and read about him or her, then write a blog post as if s/he were that person.

- *Video:* Have a video approved and ready to show to your classes. Make sure it is age-appropriate and link-able to instruction. Develop worksheets for a pre-lesson containing vocabulary and general information useful for the video, as well as post-video worksheets that will provoke discussion. It is also a good idea to have students write a reflection paragraph or essay so they can digest what they have just viewed and link it to the language, culture, and unit that has just been taught or will be taught.

Technology Malfunctions

Always be prepared for technology to fail. When your on-line video won't play or your audio file is too quiet it can be frustrating. Similarly, discovering your LCD projector bulb is out or your laptop suddenly has a virus after you worked for hours to plan the lesson makes you want to throw your device out the window. At times like these, how do you occupy your students in effective ways for the duration of the class? Here's a check list for dealing with technology malfunctions:

- Save files on a server or in the cloud, rather than directly on your laptop. That way you can retrieve them if your device crashes.
- Always test video and audio links while on the school network. Often you can access things at home on your personal network that a filter may block at work.
- When possible, download audio and video files for use in class so you are not dependent on streaming online to work every time.
- Be sure any needed devices are charged or can be plugged in during use.
- If using school devices such as tablets or laptops, be sure ahead of time that all devices are working. If you have fewer devices than students, decide in advance how you will accommodate this situation.
- If your language requires symbols and characters not used in English, make sure you know how to help students use special characters.
- In case the server in your district or at your school crashes, have an emergency lesson handy.
- Teach students to save their work often, and know where it is saved, or to work in tools that save automatically, such as Google docs. Just because they have never known life without devices does not mean they know how to save, retrieve, or submit their work.

> **?** Does your school have different network permissions for students and teachers? If so, there may be sites you can access but students are not able to. If your plan includes having students use specific online resources, be sure ahead of time that students will be able to access them.

These are just some of the many ways you can survive technology malfunctions. Probably most important is to get to know the technology experts in your school. They can be life-savers when tech quirks pop up. But don't neglect to have backup lessons at the ready, because even the tech folks get bogged down at times.

Interruptions

It is sometimes difficult to get through a day, or even a class, without an interruption of some sort. Interruptions seem to come at the most inopportune times. You may be the most organized teacher, with lesson plans outlining every minute of a class period. But when the fire alarm sounds or an emergency assembly is announced, flexibility is the name of the game. You sometimes need to make quick decisions about which activities in your lesson can be cut so you can achieve your objectives for that lesson.

At times you may lose the entire class period because of a storm or other community calamity. Remember that the students should not bear the brunt of the interruption to instruction. It is better to adjust the other classes (that are following the same lesson plan) than to expect the students from the class that experienced the interruption to do extra work.

Some teachers think they have to hurry and catch the one class up to the others, but in reality all learners can benefit from review and practice. Decide how you can give those classes time to practice what they have learned, while giving the students who missed one day time to learn the material. Teachers in areas that experience "snow days" and "late openings" are usually the most experienced in flexibility. Some winters create scenarios in which a teacher may see only second-period classes five days in a month. If you think this might happen to you, it is best to prepare students with an emergency packet that includes:

- Website links for practice

- Instructions on what students should do if they are out of school for a number of days
- Assignments on your LMS, if applicable and available for students
- Established routines so students know which resources are to be taken home daily during times when schools are closed (because of severe weather, for instance)
- Projects and research that can be completed at home when schools are closed
- Reminders that students can call a homework buddy from class so oral communication drills can be completed at home
- A check-off sheet you've developed that students can use to show what work was completed during the unexpected time away from school

> ✓ Be sure you are aware of any school policies that affect how/whether you can require assignments to be completed if students are out of school. Consider whether all students have access to online resources from home in assigning work, and if not, provide hard copies or an alternative assignment.

Whatever the cause, there may be times when school is unexpectedly closed. It is best to be prepared for such possibilities.

Student Confrontation

At some point in time during your career, you will encounter a student confrontation in one form or another. Nine times out of ten, it has less to do with you and more to do with what happened ten minutes before class, e.g., a family situation, a fight in the cafeteria, a break-up, a need to be the "attention getter" in the class, or a combination of all of the above. Learners in the class are often more affected by your reactions than by the student's actions. Keep in mind that the confrontational student wants you to react. If you put yourself at his/her level, you will lose control of the situation and the respect of the other students. It takes strength to remain calm and defuse the situation, but that will resolve it in most cases.

> ❓ What do you know about de-escalation strategies? If your answer is "not much," you need to ask colleagues, do your own research, and/or seek training on this topic.

Reprimanding students or giving ultimatums in front of their peers leaves them no way out of the contretemps. It is important for students to save face in front of their peers. You will exacerbate the situation if you demand an apology or argue with the student in front of the class. That can cost you the respect of your students, not to mention valuable class time. So to defuse a student confrontation, use techniques like these:

- In a quiet, matter-of-fact tone, say, "I know you are upset. Have a seat, and we will discuss this after class."
- You may also validate what the student is trying to say by telling him, "I hear what you are saying. Let's discuss this further after class."
- Say, "I think you need some space. Would you like to stand outside the classroom for a few minutes and come back in when you have calmed down?" This gives the student an out without having to win or lose the argument. When you are aware that the student has calmed down, you can hand that student a note suggesting remaining after class to talk with you.
- Place a chair right outside the classroom, where you can see it, give the student a legal pad, and ask that student to sit and write down what it is that is bothersome and to re-enter the classroom quietly when finished. Now you'll have the student's talking points if you need to set up a meeting after class or after school.
- If you feel the student is a danger to you or others, call the office or send a reliable student to the office to summon assistance from an administrator. Never send an upset student to the office alone.
- Do not let yourself be drawn into an argument. Remember to keep your voice calm and be in control of the situation.

When you have an opportunity to talk to a confrontational student one-on-one, you may or may not learn what triggered the outburst. But explain that in no circumstance are his/her actions acceptable, and that if it happens again you will have to call home or report it to the office. Then come up with a plan. Many schools support a contract between the teacher and the students that outlines expectations and requires monitoring and reporting regularly to parents. Your guidance counseling staff also should be able to assist with this process.

If the student should feel too upset in the near future to continue in class, that could be a signal to send (or accompany) the student to the guidance office or the clinic for "time out."

If you can find out the cause of the problem and work on a solution, most likely the student will not only appreciate your concern, but may even feel you are someone s/he can trust and confide in. However, at times a guidance counselor would be the best next step. You will not be able to solve all problems that easily, but at least you can be a facilitator in turning a bad situation around and a model for your students in how it is done.

The Unexpected Parent Visit

In most cases, if parents and guardians want to schedule a conference with you, they know to contact you in advance to set it up. After all, that information is in the kit you distributed at the beginning of the year. Depending upon the situation, it may be a good idea to have an administrator or counselor participate in the conference also.

At times parents and guardians may want to hold impromptu conferences with little or no notice, when they drop in without notice between classes or after school, want special time at Back-to-School Night or an after-school function, or happen to see you at the grocery store. If a parent comes to your classroom unannounced to talk to you, explain that you will be happy to have a conference, but to be fair to the student it is best to schedule the conference when there is enough time to discuss the situation fully. You are not obligated to talk to a parent between classes or at any unannounced time. Explain to a drop-in parent that you need time to prepare for a conference, and coordinate it with the counselor so that the outcome will benefit the student.

If a drop-in parent or guardian is simply upset about the student's grade, you may tell the person you'll call after school or in the evening to discuss the grade. In a phone call, if s/he becomes belligerent, explain politely that you will have to end the call and ask him/her to schedule a conference at a time that is convenient for both of you. If that doesn't suit the person, ask if you can reply by email. This will give the parent or guardian time to calm down and allow you time to prepare a response. If the dialogue goes beyond the issue of the student's grade, encourage the parent or guardian to come in for a conference.

The Difficult Parent Conference

Parents and guardians generally schedule parent-teacher conferences to find out how they can help their children. If you come well prepared to the conference, the meeting usually ends on a good note. You and the parents and guardians develop a plan for their child and agree to communicate periodically on the student's performance.

Some conferences may not go as smoothly as you wish. If you feel the parents and guardians are emotional about an issue, or if you have already experienced a difficult phone conversation with them, be sure to include the counselor, and even the assistant principal, in the conference. Brief the counselor and assistant principal about the out-of-control phone conversation. Ask them if you may be excused from the conference should the parent or guardian again fly off the handle during the conference. It is up to you to explain your concerns to your administrators and make sure you have their support in the event the conference gets out of hand. Nobody wants to be blindsided in a conference. As long as you talk in a calm voice, are positive, and show honest concern for the learner, your administrators should support and protect you.

Difficult Responses

In Chapter 3, communication with parents and guardians was discussed. From time to time you will receive a difficult email or letter from a parent. Writing the proper response is critical; you shouldn't answer when you are angry or emotional. Put the message aside, take some time to think about your response, and write a first draft. It is important to respond professionally and as objectively as possible. Think about how you can take the emotion out of the response to defuse the situation. Most important, avoid sarcasm in your response.

Keep these basic principles in mind when writing your final draft:

- Focus on basic good writing techniques.
- Be prompt. You do not want to inflame a situation by not addressing the concern in a timely fashion.
- Be careful. Answering criticism can be a delicate matter, even if there is no real foundation for the critic's concern or complaint.
- Neutralize the complaint.

- Answer all concerns and criticisms rationally. Don't try to "win" a verbal battle.
- Remember that every communication makes some sort of impression on the recipient, and in a sense every email or phone call is an instrument of public relations. Expect your communication to be circulated among or repeated to other parents.
- Follow this order: Think, write, rewrite, look again.
- Have someone else read your response before sending it.
- Be honest. Use only facts, and make sure they are accurate.
- Avoid educational jargon and acronyms. Some education terminology may not be understood by people outside the educational community and may cause confusion.

Format of the response:

- Make sure the reason for the correspondence comes through immediately. Begin with an opening statement that is strong and gets directly to the point.
- Create a continuing record:
  - Acknowledge the communication received from your correspondent, and refer to its date and complaint.
  - Refresh your reader's memory about a sequence of events.
  - Thank the correspondent for expressing his/her concern.
- The body of the letter or email should be direct and not wordy.
  - Set the record straight by stating facts, not by explicitly stating that the other person is "wrong."
  - If applicable, clarify what action is being taken, and why.
  - Explain the nature of the problem, what is being done about it, and what parents and guardians and students are expected to do.
  - Be tactful. Make sure your comments are judicious and courteously written. Do not agitate the reader.
- The summation should defuse the situation.
  - Display a sense of empathy. Avoid a letter that sounds form-like or bureaucratic.
  - Make the reader feel that you have taken his/her feelings, wishes, and circumstances into account. Projecting an attitude of genuine concern and acceptance of ideas is important to the success of your response.

- Closing remarks:
  - Be firm, but professional.
  - Close on a positive note, thanking the reader for his/her viewpoint.
  - Display a true sense of concern—and offer help.

It is uncommon to receive an emotional letter or email from a parent or guardian. Keep the situation in perspective. You have more than 100 students and, hopefully, have received only one emotional letter this year. Most of your parents are satisfied with what you are doing. If the parent took the time to write to you, then the concern is very important to this parent and needs your full attention. Do not dismiss a parent's concern with, "He doesn't know what he is talking about!" or "She is nuts!" Assume that every form of communication may continue on to the principal or School Board. Take a positive approach, and use this opportunity to communicate better with this parent, establish a rapport, and find mutual agreement on a solution. You will be glad you spent a little extra time responding to the difficult letter from the outset.

Medical Emergencies

Be aware of students who have any type of medical condition that may need special attention. The administration should give you a list of students in this category at the beginning of the year, or it will likely be accessible to you through an online database. If you do not get such a list, ask a colleague how to obtain this information.

You need it to react appropriately if the student should experience an allergic reaction to a bee sting, has food allergies, needs medication, or has another condition that may suddenly need your full attention. Make sure you are briefed about these students—how to spot episodes, what causes them, and how you should proceed to assist the student. For example, a teacher who did not know one of his students was diabetic sent her to the clinic alone when she complained of dizziness. On the way there, she passed out. Luckily, a teacher witnessed her collapse and immediately called for help. This critical situation could have been avoided had the teacher helped the student to the clinic at the moment she experienced dizziness.

Students' medical conditions are confidential, and you should protect their privacy by not discussing their conditions with anyone unless you have the parents' or guardians' permission or check with the school nurse. Some students are embarrassed about their conditions, and you should talk to the school nurse or counselor about how best to handle a sensitive condition. Establish a routine with each such student in your class. For example, you can allow a student who will need to visit the restroom immediately to do so without taking time to ask permission. Students who have to go to the clinic to take regularly scheduled medication may need to arrive late to class or to have hall-passes issued in advance. You might establish a signal for alerting you to an emergency situation, since time is usually a key factor in these cases.

It is harder to address classroom situations in which students without special medical conditions need to alert you to a health emergency situation. For guidance on separating legitimate emergencies from not-so-urgent needs, many teachers use the following strategies:

- Issue each student three hall passes per quarter. Each unused hall pass can be redeemed at the end of the quarter for what you feel would be a special treat. This could include fun stickers, a free homework pass, or an extra day on a project. Let it be each student's decision to use a pass without explaining its use to the teacher. A student who uses a pass with a medical explanation to the teacher would be able to receive replacement passes.
- Have a sign-in sheet at the door for any student arriving late to class. If the student was in the clinic, s/he could indicate this on the sheet, which the teacher would later check against the clinic sign-in records.
- Have brightly colored "I just want you to know …" forms for students to fill out as necessary and present to you in class. Topics on these forms might include:
  - I do not feel well and may need to go to the clinic.
  - I am upset and may need to visit my counselor.
  - I need to talk to you when you get a chance.
  - I need to use the restroom as soon as possible.

This gives you time to consider your response and fill out any appropriate forms or passes without drawing undue attention to a problem the student is experiencing. It should be understood that the nurse, counselor, or office personnel will sign your form when the student reaches the desired destination and that it will be returned to you when the student is back in the classroom. This provides you with a record of the student's whereabouts when not in your classroom.

Experiencing a Lockdown or National Emergency

There may come a time in your career when you experience a lockdown of your school. Everyone in the school will be ordered to stay put until they receive further instructions from the principal or other authority figure. Sadly, a number of schools have faced lockdowns because some students or other individuals are bent on creating mayhem in the facility. Students have been killed and injured in such situations. The lockdown could be a consequence of some sort of national emergency, which affects the community at-large. In either case, a lockdown can be a traumatic event.

> ❓ What is your school's lockdown drill procedure?

As a teacher, you may be called on to play a critical role in protecting your students. You should be prepared for such an event. Every school should have an emergency plan in the Teacher Handbook. If you haven't been briefed on this, ask your department chairperson where and how you can familiarize yourself with the plan. It usually contains detailed instructions for the teacher to follow in a variety of scenarios. Examples of teacher duties are:

- Locking your classroom doors upon hearing a prearranged announcement.
- Taking attendance and make sure all your students are present. If one or more students have left the room but are believed to be in the school, call the office immediately to report the names of students unaccounted for.
- Keeping students away from the windows.
- Not allowing students to leave the classroom until an all-clear message is received.
- Keeping students calm and quiet so directions over the loudspeaker can be heard.

Many emergency plans do not address what you should say to the students. You are told to keep the students calm, but such a situation is bound to provoke many questions and few answers in the beginning. The best you can do is to assure students that they are safe. Go over the emergency plan with them and explain that the school administration is in communication with essential personnel. Be sure you are familiar with your school's policy on students' use of cell phones, particularly during emergencies.

If students feel the situation is under control, they will stay calm. If you are panicky and nervous, you may transfer those feelings to your students, and they may be harder to control. Keep your students occupied by telling some stories or discussing a topic that should capture their attention and lessen their boredom while waiting for word about the emergency.

Remember that students look to you as their leader and will feel secure if they see that you have your wits about you. Be honest with your students and reassure them that a plan is in place. Do not let them get carried away with the "what ifs?" Stick to the facts that are known at the time. If a TV is on during a lockdown, news channel reports may be incorrect or incomplete. Some reports may sensationalize the events to the point that your students could become unglued, so check your school's emergency plan to see what it recommends in such a situation. Unfortunately, there are no perfect plans for extraordinary events like these. In the absence of clear guidance, go with your instincts and remember to make your students' safety and well-being your number one concern.

Am I ready for challenging moments?

- [ ] I have a **backup plan** always ready in case my lesson does not go as planned.
- [ ] I have planned an **extra activity** for the end of my lesson in case there is time remaining.
- [ ] I have developed a strategy to deal with **student confrontations** and am prepared to defuse the situation.
- [ ] I am prepared for any **technology malfunction**.
- [ ] I plan to save all of my work on a server or in the cloud.
- [ ] I have charged all devices or have a way to plug them in when needed.
- [ ] In case the server in my district or school crashes, I have an **emergency lesson** handy.
- [ ] I have tested video/audio files to ensure they will play correctly in the classroom.
- [ ] I have a plan in case a parent shows up **unexpectedly** for a parent conference.
- [ ] I know exactly what to do in case of a **lockdown**.
- [ ] I know all of the students in my classes that have a **medical need** or take prescription medication for a medical condition.
- [ ] I know how to **modify** a lesson or activity in case the class is interrupted and I do not have as much time remaining as I had planned.
- [ ] I am prepared to **communicate effectively** with parents and answer difficult emails or phone calls.
- [ ] I have developed **emergency lesson plans**.
  - [ ] My lessons can either be used for any class or are marked for the specific level.
  - [ ] My lessons are written so that a substitute can follow them, even if s/he does not speak the language.
  - [ ] I have provided materials and copies of handouts for the lessons and they are marked appropriately.
  - [ ] My lessons allow students to continue to learn in my absence.
- [ ] Since I am **not in one classroom** for all my classes, I have developed a system to help me stay organized while I travel.
  - [ ] I have worked out a system with the teacher who also uses the classroom.
  - [ ] I have a bookcase, a table, a section of the bulletin board or wall space, a drawer of a file cabinet, a shelf of a wardrobe, drop boxes, and/or a file folder stand to store my materials.
  - [ ] I have a traveling cart with room for all my materials for each class.

Reflection

What aspects of this chapter worked well?

What would I change for next year?

How would I change it?

What additional resources do I need to gather for next year?

Template T
Emergency Lesson Plan 1

High School

Emergency Lesson Plan: Multiple Levels

Dear Substitute,

Students can use this choice board to select their activities. They must turn in all three activities, and these will be graded. Thank you for taking care of my classes today!

Me llamo _____ *Fecha* _____ *Clase* _____

Directions: Choose any three (3) of the activities below: you must do three across, three up and down, or three diagonally. Spend about 25-30 minutes on each activity. Be sure to circle the activities you have chosen and attach any papers to this grid.

Write an acrostic poem about yourself in Spanish, using your first and last name. Your poem must have at least 30 total words in it. You may use a dictionary to help you find words if needed. If you use a word that is new to you, include a small illustration beside it.	On YouTube or Spotify, listen to at least three (3) songs by the same Spanish-speaking music artist (could be Juanes, Ozuna, Enrique Iglesias, Shakira, or any other artist you find). Write the title and artist of each song and a three-sentence reaction: What did you think of each song? How did it make you feel? What words did you understand?	Research a holiday in a Spanish-speaking country, and create a colorful poster on a piece of printer paper. Your poster should explain the name of the holiday, when it is celebrated, why it is celebrated, and how it is celebrated. Include at least one relevant illustration.
Create a poster on a piece of printer paper advertising or explaining a product that is sold in a Spanish-speaking country but nonexistent in the U.S.. Be sure to show the name of the product, what it looks like, what it is used for, and how much it costs.	Research a current event in México. Go to news.google.com or news.google.com.mx (you can search for "México" and browse the stories). Write down the title and source of the article, a five-sentence summary of what you read, and a five-sentence reaction (including your opinion).	Browse amazon.com.mx for at least 10 different items you could purchase. Write a list of the items you found, and include the following information for each: name of item, price, description of item (what does it do, or what it is used for?), and summarize at least one written review of the item (what did the writer think of it?)
Compare languages! Write a list of 10 vocabulary words you know (write the English word and then the Spanish translation). Then look up and write down each word in French, Portuguese, Italian, and German. Write five sentences explaining any similarities and differences among the languages and why you think those similarities and differences exist.	Write a script for a conversation related to our current unit. Your conversation should have at least two people, and each person should have at least 10 lines. Use (and be sure to circle) at least three vocabulary words and/or grammar concepts in your conversation.	Write an itinerary for a three-day trip to a Spanish-speaking city. For each day of your trip, list two activities or attractions and two places to eat. Explain why you chose each of the places you did and how much each activity or meal will cost.

Template U | Emergency Lesson Plan 2

High
School

Emergency Lesson Plan: Level 3

All the materials for this lesson are in this manila envelope. Please do not worry if you do not speak the target language. The students will be able to work collaboratively in groups.

High Spanish 3 Theme: Environment Topic: Ecology

Targeted standards:

Objective:
- Students will ask and answer questions about ecology.

Essential learning:
- Students will understand and produce vocabulary related to ecological issues.
- Students will ask and answer questions related to conservation.
- Students will incorporate the conditional mood into their communication using clauses with "should."

How this lesson connects with what has already been learned:
- Students have created posters on ecology prior to this lesson. The posters are posted on the wall. The students may use the posters to generate ideas. Students will use the learned vocabulary when producing a children's book on ecology.
- Students will use a graphic organizer to capture learned words and phrases related to ecological issues and conservation.

How to engage the student:
- Tell students that today they will start writing a 20-page children's book on ecology and conservation. They will be able to ask and answer questions about the ecology and conservation.
- Have students share ideas about how one should present information to 6-year-old children.

Today's lesson:
- Ask students to form groups of four and distribute the handouts, which include instructions.
- Each student will have an assignment: (1) recorder, (2) editor, (3) illustrator, (4) publisher.
- Ask students to brainstorm how they want to present the information to children.
- Ask students to clarify their findings by responding to a few questions provided in the handout.
- Hand each group a packet of 20 sheets of blank paper, and ask them to create a draft of the questions/answers that will go on each page.
- The students will have the following responsibilities:
  - The **recorder** will write down the ideas for each page.
  - The **illustrator** will suggest pictures/images that should be included.
  - The **editor** will edit the language structures, content, and vocabulary.
  - The **publisher** will arrange the content and decide on the layout of the book.

Reflection:
- Have students consult their textbooks (and authentic material provided in this packet) for any ecology/conservation expressions they forgot to include.
- Have students think about ecological issues in Spanish-speaking countries.

How this lesson affects the next lesson:
Explain that the next lesson will be devoted to completing the book and peer editing. When the project is finished, the students will send the books to the neighboring elementary school that has a large Spanish-speaking population for display in its library.

Materials included in this packet:

- Posters with vocabulary related to ecology and conservation instruction packets for each student
- Authentic articles on ecology (that have already been discussed)
- Packets of 20 blank sheets (one per group)
- Rubric on how the project will be assessed

Chapter 5 | How Do I Grow?

There is so much to learn during your first year! It is important to celebrate your accomplishments, but it is also essential to reflect on the school year and develop a plan to refine your teaching strategies so your next year can be even better.

Where should you begin? This chapter will guide your analysis of what worked, what needs more attention, and what resources are available to help you through the rest of your career. The skillful teacher is a lifelong learner, always striving to improve. It is important to change with your clientele and stay current on new practices. You'll find that what worked one year may not work the next. Be flexible and be prepared to research best practices, review what you created, revise what was not effective, refine what worked well, and keep an open mind regarding change.

Continuous Improvement

Continual learning and reflection will keep your teaching career strong and enjoyable. Just like a surgeon, lawyer, or engineer, you must stay current with new research and developments in your field. Attend workshops, seminars, and demonstrations; collaborate with colleagues on learning; and involve yourself in improvement programs.

Above all, embrace change; it energizes thinking. Prepare yourself each year to greet learners with different strengths, varied abilities, diverse backgrounds, distinct needs, and a variety of learning styles. If you just pull last year's lesson plans out of your files without refining them to meet the needs of this new group of individuals, you will soon be scratching your head wondering why something that worked marvelously last year is not working at all this year.

If you assess each year to learn how to be better prepared for the next, not only will you develop a wealth of resources, but you will also sharpen your teaching techniques to meet the needs of the ever-changing student population in today's society.

Reflections:

When you review your past year, reassess your goals and objectives for that year:

- Did you meet your goals?
- Did you meet your objectives?
- What are your indicators?
- What evidence do you have that you met your goals and objectives?

Analyze each aspect of the past year by quarter or by grading period. Go through your unit and lesson plans to see what notations you made along the way. Use the following questions to rate your performance:

Assessments:

- Did I have to reassess because most of my students did not score as well as I had hoped on the previous assessment? *(List the assessments as a reminder.)*
- Did the assessments actually measure the intended learning objective? *(If not, list the ones that need revision.)*
- Did I vary the assessments to measure not only content information but also interpersonal communication, presentational and interpretive abilities, cultural knowledge, and informal use of the language?
- How often did I assess? *(The fewer grades you have, the heavier the weight each one has).*
- Did my grades really measure what the learners were able to do?
- Did I feel at any time that the quarter grade was off the mark?
- Were my assessments aligned with those of my colleagues?
- Did I collaborate with teachers who teach the same language and level that I do?
- Do I know if all students were given equal opportunities to speak in class? Did my class participation grade really measure this?

- How did I address all three modes of communication in my instruction and assessment (Interpretive, Interpersonal, Presentational)?

Lesson plans:

- Which lessons were my most successful ones? Why?
- Which lessons created confusion? Why?
- Which lessons took the most time to complete?
- Which lessons needed the least time to complete?
- Which theme or topic needs more emphasis based on the results seen on assessments?
- Do I need to pace myself better?
- Did I spend too much time on some topics and not enough on others?
- Is there a topic or language structure I did not address?
- Did I have to speed up at the end of the year to get everything in?

Balance:

- Were my classes more teacher-centered, or more student-centered?
- Did I vary my instructional practices?
- Did I give my students enough opportunity to use the language in interpersonal communication? Did my assessments measure their progress in this area?
- Was enough time spent on having students listen to native speakers of the language? Did I assess interpretive listening often enough?
- Am I satisfied with how many opportunities I gave my students to read authentic material? Did I teach my students to access authentic resources?
- How often did I require my students to write?
- At the end of the year, could my students write on their own without a "check list" of what they were to include?
- Did I teach my students the writing process, or did I expect them to already know how to write?

Communication with students, parents, and guardians:

- How often did parents and guardians call me saying they needed more clarification of my expectations?
- How often did students tell me they didn't know I was going to assess certain aspects of the chapter or thematic unit?

- How often did students not turn things in because they didn't know those assignments were due?
- How often did students fail to make up missed work?
- How often did students come unprepared for the day's lesson?
- Did I communicate with parents and guardians in a timely manner?
- Did I fail to inform the parents of any students who had dropped two letter grades before the end of the grading period?

Homework:

- Did my students complain that my homework assignments were just "busy work?"
- Did my assignments enable students to practice what was taught during the class period?
- How frequently did students comment that they didn't understand homework assignments? Which ones?
- Did I ever use homework or grade homework as punishment?

Classroom management:

- What do I need to establish at the beginning of the year that I did not do this year?
- Did my students show me respect?
- Did I have to bribe my students to get them to do what I wanted?
- Did I issue ultimatums? If so, did I follow through on them?
- Was I consistent in implementing my classroom rules?
- How often did I have to tell my class to pay attention?
- Did I have the attention of all of my students when I was teaching, or did I have to talk over them?
- Did the students understand and follow my classroom routines? If not, was it because I didn't have routines firmly established?

Staff development and training:

- How did I take advantage of staff development opportunities?
- How often did I collaborate with my colleagues?
- Did I ask questions, or did I try to figure out things on my own?

- Did I seek help from my department chairperson or mentor?
- Did I read any professional journals or research during the year that helped me?
- Did I use all of the resources available to me?

After completing a self-assessment of your first year, the next step is to develop a plan for the following year. Identify areas of need so you can devote time and study to them before the new school year begins. You will be amazed at how much concentration you can give to the curriculum when you have no school year distractions.

Revisions for Next Year

After identifying areas that need revision or refinement, prioritize your improvement goals. Every area mentioned in the preceding section affects student achievement, but if you look at your answers in each section, does one area stand out above the others? If so, you will want to make this a priority area for improvement for the following year. As you consider professional goal-setting for next year, reflect on what went well or not so well this year, and consider the reasons for that, so you can maintain effective practices and make adjustments where needed.

✔ Use the TELL framework and related documents to reflect on your practice and set goals for next year. (See Appendix E.)

On the other hand, you may feel that your students achieved what you thought they *should* throughout the year but you want to vary your assessments to include more speaking performance assessments next year. Then you need to examine your answers in the Balance section above to see if you were giving learners enough opportunity to perform during class time. Your priority list would show the following areas of focus:

1. Revise lesson plans to allow more time for partner activities to improve interpersonal communication.
2. Ask learners to use a rubric to rate themselves on a performance task to better understand expectations.
3. Develop multiple speaking performance assessments per unit.

4. Allow time for learners to set goals and keep a portfolio to chart progress on performance assessments. Use the *NCSSFL-ACTFL Can-Do Statements* to help students be aware of their learning.

Likewise, if classroom management is an area you have identified for improvement, develop an improvement plan. The following suggestions are recommended:

- Participate in summer workshops that focus on classroom management strategies.
- Ask the administration if you can have release time during the last month of school to observe a teacher who is recognized for having good classroom management skills. (This is usually a time when students can be rather challenging. You will pick up excellent strategies during times full of distractions.)
- Ask a colleague to observe you during his/her planning period before the end of the school year. Sit down with this teacher and take note of what s/he has to say. Don't be defensive. Remember, it is hard to see what habits we have formed while teaching.
- Give your students an evaluation survey form at the end of the year. They will usually take the time to express their opinions, indicating areas of satisfaction and frustrations with the course. Read between the lines, and use this information to your benefit.

When you have gathered the data you need to make revisions, develop a plan and stick to it. If you discover the need to be more consistent, only make rules you can enforce with every student all the time. Go back over your class rules and see if they need modifications. If the administration failed to back you up on a certain rule, revise it to make it consistent with school policy.

Be certain that you list the essential elements needing revisions for continued success. It is easy to get sidetracked and spend the whole summer redesigning your bulletin board when assessments should be your real focus. Don't be afraid to ask for advice. See if colleagues have helpful material they are willing to share. You do not want to reinvent the wheel.

✔ Share your reflection and goal setting with a mentor or colleague. S/he can be helpful in working toward your goals for next year.

Successful Solutions

Nobody can give you solutions to every problem, but there are resources out there to help you find them. I often hear new teachers say, "If only I had known s/he could have helped me. The information was there all along, but I didn't have time to look through all the ancillaries during the school year." Or "I can't believe I created all of this from scratch and later found out my colleague had something similar I could have used."

The following tips may lead you to some solutions you have been looking for:

- Find out early what your teaching assignment will be for next year, and collaborate with a veteran teacher before the school year ends.
- Check with curriculum specialists in the central office of your district about any workshops planned for the fall of the next school year.
- Collaborate with teachers who have taught the level above the one you will teach next year, so you have a clear picture of where you want your students to be at the end of next year.
- Check the Internet for any educational research that might lead you to strategies that can assist in teaching certain topics and getting the best results out of your students.
- Go to your professional library to read educational journals that address your areas of concern.
- Get involved in summer curriculum projects that let you connect with teachers from other schools and exchange ideas. Though you are a new teacher, some projects can use your input and creativity.
- Look for summer professional development opportunities.
- Check to see what course offerings are available at local colleges or universities.
- Look through the bookroom at your school for additional resources that may be tucked away from previous years.
- Ask teachers who have recently retired if they would be willing to donate their materials to your school. (Always evaluate such materials to ensure alignment with current standards and curricula.)
- Check with your PTA president to see if funds are available to purchase materials that you have identified as necessary for your program.
- Check with the media specialist to see if funds are available to add reading material or other authentic resources for students in the target language.
- Collaborate with teachers in other disciplines to see if they have materials you can use to enrich your curriculum.
- Check the elementary resources for materials you can use for your beginning language classes. (Many posters and handouts used at that level can be very useful in your courses, though you may need to label the target language over the English).
- Visit teacher stores, and be inventive about finding materials available in other subjects that can be used in a language class.

Teacher Evaluation and Observations

Most school systems have established procedures for teacher evaluation. The evaluation process is key to your growth as a professional educator. Find out early in the year what those procedures are, and learn how you will be evaluated. Generally, a goal-setting conference is held early in the year with your evaluator, and this will be an opportunity for you to ask questions about the process. You can always ask your department chair about how the process will work in your school.

You may be asked to provide the following information regarding your lesson:

- National, state, and local standards
- Planning and assessment
- Instruction
- Learning environment

Develop lesson plans to include the Standards:
(See *World-Readiness Standards for Learning Languages,* Appendix B)

- Communication—Interpretive, Interpersonal, and Presentational Modes
- Cultures
- Connections
- Comparisons
- Communities

Plan lessons that:

- Integrate listening, speaking, reading, and writing into the three modes of communication.
- Are student-centered, which includes working independently, in pairs, or in groups.
- Recognize a diverse student population.
- Include a variety of learning modes.
- Provide opportunities for practice.
- Are aligned with the district's curriculum guide and are not textbook-driven.

If you have a pre-observation conference:

- Tell the observer what you expect the students to learn at the end of the lesson.
- Explain to the observer what students have learned in the previous lesson.
- Show the observer what you have planned for the next lesson.
- Make sure you indicate to the observer how your lesson is aligned with standards.
- Indicate to the observer how students will be assessed throughout the lesson.
- Explain to the observer how the lesson aligns with unit goals.

What administrators may look for:

- You and the students speaking the target language throughout the lesson in Level 1 through Upper Level. The ACTFL Core Practice is 90%+ target language use by teachers and students at all levels. (See Guiding Principles and Core Practices, Appendix D.)
- Students speaking the language at every opportunity. (Student performance is the focus.)
- Using strategies for providing comprehensible input, such as visual cues, motions, repetition, and cognates, instead of using English to enhance learning.
- Using the textbook as a resource but not as the sole source of information.
- Using a variety of strategies to meet the needs of all learners.
- Students practicing with partners often. (A noisy class is not a bad class.)
- Assessing students often and in a variety of ways, formally and informally.

- Effective use of digital tools/resources for the learning or assessment goals.

Learning Environment:

- The classroom climate must be positive in mood and presentation.
- Students must feel it is "safe" to make a mistake.
- Students must show respect toward other students and allow for mistakes.
- Desks are arranged to allow for communication.
- Students feel no question is a dumb question, and participation is encouraged.
- Teachers encourage students constantly.

Assessments should:

- Assess what has been learned in the class.
- Be used frequently and in a variety of ways.
- Include formative performance assessments.
- Include summative performance assessments.

> **(?)** What is the evaluation and observation process in your school or district? It may be different for beginning teachers than for veteran teachers.

Professional Organizations

Involvement with your state, regional and/or national professional associations is extremely important for your professional growth. These organizations have a wealth of resources to share, and hold excellent conferences. If you've never been to one, you don't know what you're missing! In fact, most of these conferences offer many workshops on topics that can benefit all language educators.

> **(?)** What professional organizations are available to you? What are your state and regional professional language organizations? When are their conferences?

Vendors display a variety of supplemental materials that can aid classroom teachers. Publishers often have all of the ancillaries on display and will demonstrate their usefulness. Sometimes vendors give out free samples of classroom materials and products that you can try out in your classroom. Of course, they come with order forms, catalogues, and vendors' business cards, in the interest of keeping you in touch with them.

A key aspect of conferences is the networking you can do with colleagues in your field. You often see teachers trading email addresses and promising to send one another material. Conference workshops usually reserve time for questions and discussion, and your questions can often be answered by experts in the field and discussed with colleagues from far and wide.

Teaching is not a solitary experience. You have to learn from others! Teaching is all about collaborating, sharing, and borrowing ideas. You can develop an amazing network of colleagues by attending conferences and becoming involved in professional organizations. Most of them offer members a wealth of services: publications, research data, professional development opportunities, scholarships, competitions, testing services, listservs, study abroad opportunities, advocacy committees, etc. Explore the website for your state and regional associations.

Conference information is readily available months in advance of the actual event. Session descriptions can be viewed before a conference so teachers can see what is offered that might help them. Hotel and travel prices are usually discounted for conference attendees. If registration, hotel, travel, and meals come to more than your budget can afford, there may be sources of support. For example, many school districts will pay for either teachers' conference registration and/or substitute day teachers attending the conference. Many organizations provide special pricing for new teachers or first-time attendees.

Teachers sometimes forget that a school's PTA might have funds that can offset the cost of conferences. You may need to submit a proposal and a request for the entire amount and see what's available for you. Ask your school administration if funds are set aside for staff development. Be prepared to offer turn-around training upon your return. The cost of sending you to a conference can benefit the entire department. It is surprising that many teachers do not ask for assistance. But it will cost you nothing to apply for it, and the payoff can be just what you need.

Credit for attending a conference is also a real bonus. Check with your school system and make sure you understand what types of professional development are required for recertification. Generally all conferences are approved for required points. Before attending a conference, find out what you will need to document your attendance. After attending a conference or two, you may want to submit a proposal to present a workshop on your own. If you have a lesson or materials that you find very successful, you'll certainly want to share your strategies with your colleagues!

Professional Learning Network

Developing a professional learning network (PLN) also helps you grow professionally. A PLN includes colleagues to collaborate with, blogs to follow, social media accounts to follow on Twitter, Facebook, Instagram, etc. A PLN enables you to constantly learn from people you don't even know! When you attend professional conferences, you will find presenters and colleagues from whom you can learn. Make them a part of your PLN by following them on social media! Professional groups on social media have online chat sessions and spaces for sharing ideas and resources. You can participate in groups that are language-specific as well as those that address language teaching in general. Developing a PLN allows you to learn from colleagues, those near and far, in different ways and on your schedule. The best part is that a PLN is free!

Overseas Travel/Educational Trips

A student trip to your target language country can be a marvelous experience for you and your students. You can imagine the value of using what you have learned in the classroom with peers who are natives of the country. On such a trip, even students who have practiced the language and learned about the culture for several years exclaim, "The houses really do look like this!" as the tour bus weaves through the countryside. Students do not think you made it all up—but the culture and language do not become a reality until they are there, looking at everything that was just a picture in a book prior to the trip.

One of a language teacher's greatest joys is to watch students interact with local residents, shopkeepers, bus drivers, etc., and manage on their own the language skills you taught them. Most of these educational travel opportunities are package tours with guides who remain with the group for the entire trip. Travel is prearranged and includes sightseeing excursions with local guides who tell the history of the places you visit. These tours usually include hotel accommodations, transportation, museum and historic site entrance tickets, guides, and most meals. Trips like these can take a year to plan in cooperation with parents and other supporters.

With an enterprise this ambitious, you'll want to heed some caveats before you agree to take students overseas:

- Have an experienced teacher travel with you to help shepherd your students. Make sure that teacher has traveled abroad with students before.
- Have one adult chaperone for every five or six students, and assign each adult responsibility for the same students for the entire trip.
- Have a photocopy of every student's passport on hand before you depart, and throughout the trip.
- Conduct passport checks three or four times a day. Just ask students to hold their passport up so you can see them every time you are about to pull away in the bus.
- Never allow students to drink alcohol in another country away from their parents and guardians, even with parent or guardian permission. Everyone reacts to alcohol differently, and an adverse reaction could have you taking a student to a hospital or bailing one out of jail and leaving you facing a lawsuit. Many teachers have expressed regret at allowing students to have "just one" glass of beer or wine at dinner. It is not worth a lawsuit just to have a minor "experience" the culture to this degree in another country. This is a school trip, so school rules apply, regardless of the country's laws.
- Make sure students and parents understand the rules before departing. Do not hesitate to send a student home if s/he endangers him/herself or the group.
- Encourage students to have a budget so that they know exactly how much they can spend each day on souvenirs, food, beverages, etc.

- Use a well-established tour company with insurance covering cancellation, illness, lost luggage, and travel interruptions.
- Make sure you read every line of the contract, explain everything precisely to parents and guardians, and arrange extensive personal liability insurance coverage.

Trips like these can be very rewarding if well planned and organized. Bumps in the road can come with misunderstanding the contract (what is covered, what isn't covered, handling tipping, etc.). Students will remember the experience for a long time to come. Your first experience taking students abroad will also be rewarding if you prepare for the unknown well in advance.

Exchange programs are another means of overseas travel for students. They usually stay in a host family's home for three weeks to a year, depending on the program. These experiences give students true insight into a country's people, culture, and language. Not only are these students able to fine-tune their language ability, but they also have experiences that could never be replicated in a classroom. Generally the students from the host country will come to the United States to stay with your students for a similar period of time. Bonds created in these programs can last a lifetime.

> ✅ Be sure to investigate school/district policies regarding international trips before embarking on such a venture!

Am I prepared for professional growth?

☐ I have answered this chapter's questions regarding the past year.

☐ After answering the questions, I know what I want to do differently next year, and what I want to keep the same.

☐ I have used the teacher evaluation process as an opportunity for learning and improvement.

☐ I have begun to establish a PLN, connecting with colleagues (known and unknown) through social media outlets.

☐ I plan to join a professional organization.

☐ I plan to attend conferences and be a presenter at one or more.

☐ I plan to seek some type of leadership role within the school community.

☐ I plan to research opportunities for my students to gain additional exposure to native speakers of the target language.

Reflection

What aspects of this year were successful?

What is the first thing I plan to revise or refine for next year?

How should I revise it?

What outside resources do I have available to me to accomplish this?

How do I plan to get more involved on a local, regional, or national level?

Appendix A | Oral Proficiency Levels in the Workplace

ACTFL Level	ILR	Language Functions	Corresponding Professions/Positions	Examples of Who is Likely to Function at This Level
Distinguished	5 / 4	Ability to tailor language to specific audience, persuade, negotiate. Deal with nuance and subtlety.	Foreign Service Diplomat, Contract Negotiator, International Specialist, Intelligence Specialist	• Highly articulate, professionally specialized native speakers • Language learners with extended (17 years) and current professional and/or educational experience in the target culture
Superior	3	Discuss topics extensively, support opinions, hypothesize. Deal with linguistically unfamiliar situation.	University Language Professor, Financial Services Marketing Consultant, Foreign Area Officer, Lawyer, Judge, Court Interpreter	• Well-educated native speakers • Educated language learners with extended professional and/or educational experience in the target language environment
Advanced High	2+ / 2	Narrate and describe in past, present and future and deal effectively with an unanticipated complication	Physician, Human Resources Communications Consultant, Financial Services Senior Consultant, Quality Assurance Specialist, Marketing Manager, Financial Advisor, Broker, Military Linguist, Translation Officer	• Language learners with graduate degrees in language or a related area and extended educational experience in target environment
Advanced Mid			Banking and Investment Services Customer Service Representative, Fraud Specialist, Account Executive, Medical Interpreter, Patient Advocate, Court Stenographer, Court Interpreter, Human Resources Benefits Specialist, Technical Service Agent, Collection Representative, Estimating Coordinator	• Heritage speakers, informal learners, non-academic learners who have significant contact with language • Undergraduate majors with year-long study in the target language culture
Advanced Low			K–12 Language Teacher, Nurse, Social Worker, Claims Processor, Police Officer, Maintenance Administrator, Billing Clerk, Legal Secretary, Legal Receptionist. 911 Dispatcher, Consumer Products Customer Services Representative, Retail Services Personnel	• Undergraduate language majors
Intermediate High	1+	Create with language, initiate, maintain and bring to a close simple conversations by asking and responding to simple questions	Firefighter, Utilities Installer, Auto Inspector, Aviation Personnel, Missionary, Tour Guide	• Language learners following 6-8 year sequences of study (AP, etc.) or 4-6 semester college sequence
Intermediate Mid	1		Cashier, Sales clerk (highly predictable contexts), Receptionist	
Intermediate Low				• Language learners following four-year high-school sequence or two-semester college sequence • Language learners following an immersion language program in grades K–6
Novice High	0+	Communicate minimally with formulaic and rote utterances, lists and phrases	*The levels of proficiency associated with each of the positions above are minimal levels of oral proficiency based on task analyses.*	• Language learners following content-based language program in grades K–6
Novice Mid	0		*The minimal levels were determined by subject matter experts from companies and agencies who use ACTFL proficiency tests.*	• Language learners following two years of high-school language study
Novice Low				

©2015 *American Council on the Teaching of Foreign Languages*

Appendix B | World-Readiness Standards

GOAL AREAS	STANDARDS		
COMMUNICATION Communicate effectively in more than one language in order to function in a variety of situations and for multiple purposes	**Interpersonal Communication:** Learners interact and negotiate meaning in spoken, signed, or written conversations to share information, reactions, feelings, and opinions.	**Interpretive Communication:** Learners understand, interpret, and analyze what is heard, read, or viewed on a variety of topics.	**Presentational Communication:** Learners present information, concepts, and ideas to inform, explain, persuade, and narrate on a variety of topics using appropriate media and adapting to various audiences of listeners, readers, or viewers.
CULTURES Interact with cultural competence and understanding	**Relating Cultural Practices to Perspectives:** Learners use the language to investigate, explain, and reflect on the relationship between the practices and perspectives of the cultures studied.	**Relating Cultural Products to Perspectives:** Learners use the language to investigate, explain, and reflect on the relationship between the products and perspectives of the cultures studied.	
CONNECTIONS Connect with other disciplines and acquire information and diverse perspectives in order to use the language to function in academic and career-related situations	**Making Connections:** Learners build, reinforce, and expand their knowledge of other disciplines while using the language to develop critical thinking and to solve problems creatively.	**Acquiring Information and Diverse Perspectives:** Learners access and evaluate information and diverse perspectives that are available through the language and its cultures.	
COMPARISONS Develop insight into the nature of language and culture in order to interact with cultural competence	**Language Comparisons:** Learners use the language to investigate, explain, and reflect on the nature of language through comparisons of the language studied and their own.	**Cultural Comparisons:** Learners use the language to investigate, explain, and reflect on the concept of culture through comparisons of the cultures studied and their own.	
COMMUNITIES Communicate and interact with cultural competence in order to participate in multilingual communities at home and around the world	**School and Global Communities:** Learners use the language both within and beyond the classroom to interact and collaborate in their community and the globalized world.	**Lifelong Learning:** Learners set goals and reflect on their progress in using languages for enjoyment, enrichment, and advancement.	

Appendix C | NCSSFL-ACTFL Can-Do Statements

The 2017 *NCSSFL-ACTFL Can-Do Statements*, the result of collaboration between the National Council of State Supervisors for Languages (NCSSFL) and the American Council on the Teaching of Foreign Languages (ACTFL), guide the following people:

- Language learners, to identify and set learning goals and chart their progress toward language and intercultural proficiency;
- Educators, to write communication learning targets for curriculum, unit and lesson plans;
- Stakeholders, to clarify how well learners at different stages can communicate.

The statements are organized according to the Interpretive, Interpersonal, and Presentational Modes of Communication as described in the *World-Readiness Standards for Learning Languages*:

- *Interpretive Communication:* Learners understand, interpret, and analyze what is heard, read, or viewed on a variety of topics.
- *Interpersonal Communication:* Learners interact and negotiate meaning in spoken, signed, or written conversations to share information, reactions, feelings, and opinions.
- *Presentational Communication:* Learners present information, concepts, and ideas to inform, explain, persuade, and narrate on a variety of topics, using appropriate media and adapting to various audiences of listeners, readers, or viewers.

How *The NCSSFL-ACTFL Can-Do Statements* Are Organized

Proficiency Benchmarks

Identify the overarching features of language performance, i.e., context, text type, and function, in each of the three modes of communication to describe learner's progress along the ACTFL Proficiency continuum. Benchmarks support learners in setting long-term goals and inform program and course outcomes.

Performance Indicators

Deconstruct the Benchmark by focusing on certain aspects of language performance, i.e., context, text type, and function. Indicators describe the steps toward reaching the overarching Benchmark goal. Indicators support learners in charting progress toward meeting language learning goals and inform unit design.

Examples

Illustrate language performance in a variety of learning contexts (e.g., social, academic across PK–20, immersion, adult) and inform instruction at the lesson or learning activity level.

All information regarding the Can-Do Statements and the related documents can be found at: https://www.actfl.org/publications/guidelines-and-manuals/ncssfl-actfl-can-do-statements.

Appendix D | Guiding Principles and Core Practices for World Language Learning

The American Council on the Teaching of Foreign Languages has developed Guiding Principles for effective language learning. These inform not just educators and learners but also all stakeholders: parents, administrators, governing bodies/boards, legislators, the community at large, etc. This initial set of statements comes from the position statements previously approved by the ACTFL Board; it is not a finite or fixed list. This set of statements will evolve and continue to grow as new topics emerge and to reflect new realities in the diversity of learners and learning situations. These statements respond to the challenge to identify what is effective in language learning and to guide educators and learners. ACTFL welcomes ongoing discussion to update and refine these statements, informed by new research and experiences.

These Guiding Principles provide the means to shape discussion to answer questions that arise about specific practices, policies, or programs. Professional learning communities or networks (including language departments, online communities, and formal or informal groups) will use these statements to explore their practices for language instruction and assessment. Non-educators (including parents, board members, and administrators) will use these statements as a description of what to observe in classrooms at any level and a set of criteria for discussing what is effective for language learning.

The Guiding Principles include:

1. Benefits of Language Learning
2. Literacy in Language Learning
3. Articulated Sequences in Language Learning
4. Use of Target Language in Language Learning (Core Practice: Facilitate Target Language Comprehensibility)
5. Use of Authentic Texts in Language Learning (Core Practice: Guide Learners through Interpreting Authentic Resources)
6. Designing Oral Communication Tasks for Language Learning (Core Practice: Design Oral Interpersonal Communication Tasks)
7. Backward Design Planning Model for Language Learning (Core Practice: Plan with Backward Design Model)
8. Teaching Grammar as Concepts in Meaningful Contexts in Language Learning (Core Practice: Teach Grammar as Concept and Use in Context)
9. Critical Role of Feedback in Language Learning (Core Practice: Provide Appropriate Oral Feedback)

The full document and an explanation of each principle can be found at www.actfl.org/guiding-principles.

ACTFL's Core Practices are essential for effective language instruction. These research-based strategies are the anchor components of appropriate pedagogy in the world language classroom. These practices are well explained in various methods texts and other resources, including the online resources ACTFL provides. Additional suggested resources include *Languages and Children: Making the Match* (2015, Curtain and Dahlberg), *Teacher's Handbook: Contextualized Language Instruction* (2015, Shrum & Glisan), and *The Keys to Planning for Learning: Effective Curriculum, Unit, and Lesson Design (second edition)* (2017, Clementi & Terrill). ACTFL online modules can be found at www.actfl.org.

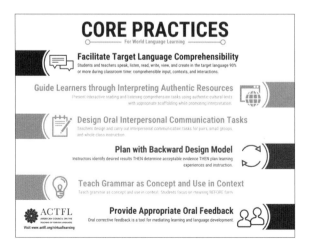

Appendix E | Reflection and Self-Assessment: The TELL Framework

The Teacher Effectiveness for Language Learning (TELL) Framework was developed to identify model teacher characteristics and behaviors for world language educators. The framework, tools, and resources are designed to help teachers identify strengths and opportunities for growth. Self-assessment and peer observation tools can be used in a variety of ways, including self-reflection and goal setting, and can benefit teachers of any experience level. The domains and criteria are research-based, and aligned with other frameworks of effective instruction. The TELL Framework is specifically designed for language educators, incorporating ACTFL's Six Core Practices and research based pedagogy, helping teachers to approach professional improvement from a growth mindset. (See www.tellproject.org for the self-assessment tools, feedback/peer observation tools, and links to other resources, including videos.)

TELL Framework

Preparing for Student Learning:
- Environment
- Planning

Advancing Student Learning:
- The Learning Experience
- Performance & Feedback
- Learning Tools

Supporting Student Learning:
- Collaboration
- Professionalism

Feedback Tools

- Checking for Understanding
- Facilitating Learner Interactions
- Giving Directions & Modeling
- Learner Engagement
- Learning Tools/Resources
- Pair & Small Group Work
- Physical Environment
- Target Language Use (Student)
- Target Language Use (Teacher)

Afterword

When you ask first-year language teachers why they chose education, the response usually sounds something like this: "I wanted to make a difference in the lives of kids and instill in them a love of language learning." Similarly, when you attend a retirement reception to honor an educator who has devoted his/her life to education, retirees often reflect on events associated with specific students who made their entire careers worthwhile. One can conclude, then, that educators never lose the desire to be a positive force in their students' lives. Their drive to make an impact on the lives of others constitutes the bedrock of why they became involved in education in the first place. Those who have successful careers in the field keep their focus and reflect on the difference they have made in the lives of students and colleagues. For some novice teachers, however, the ideal becomes clouded by the day-to-day demands and pressures of teaching.

It is well documented that many teachers entering the profession leave within the first few years and never return. Why? Is having the desire to influence the lives of students not enough? What role can veterans play in helping to keep others in the profession? We are all familiar with stories of teachers who start their careers with boundless energy and creative ideas and quickly become disillusioned with duties and responsibilities that seemingly have little or nothing to do with classroom instruction and individual students.

The reasons most often given for leaving the profession are also known. Some cite lack of support from their peers and administrators; others are overwhelmed by the workload. Still others say their backgrounds and training did not adequately prepare them for the demands of being a classroom teacher. Language teachers are also often disappointed that not all of their students are passionate about learning another language and culture. Still others comment on perceived student apathy and misbehavior. The list goes on and on and should serve as a call to action to those of us who are devoting our lives to this profession.

What can we do to assist those newest to teaching? Career language educators must discover how to support and to mentor new teachers more effectively. Just as the most effective teachers are reflective practitioners who constantly strive to improve their practice, veteran educators must reflect on filling the needs of our profession as a whole. Many of us who have "made it" past those critical first few years can point to one or two colleagues who took us under their wing and helped us deal with the seemingly endless issues we faced during that first year in the classroom.

For example, during my first year of teaching, a special colleague spent countless hours helping me to plan lessons, troubleshooting problems with a test I spent hours developing, and giving me a heads up about important deadlines throughout the year. At the same time, this colleague used a number of activity ideas I suggested, which made me feel like I was giving something back to her for all the time she spent helping me.

Mentoring means more than showing the new teacher where the photocopier is and how to use the electronic gradebook. It means developing a mutually beneficial, ongoing, professional relationship. The novice teacher can energize the veteran teacher with new ideas, while the veteran teacher helps to anticipate roadblocks and listens critically to the highs and lows in order to encourage new educators to think critically about their lessons and interactions with students.

Current language teachers must also recruit their students to become language teachers. Some students will be attracted to our profession if they recognize and sense the enthusiasm and passion we have for teaching languages. Students size up their teachers quickly and know which ones genuinely enjoy what they do.

Given the critical need for language teachers, however, we may need to more directly point out to students the reasons to become a language teacher. Talk to your students about why you became a teacher and what you like most about it. Encourage students to practice teaching the language they are learning with friends, family, and others. Explain the travel benefits and ongoing lifelong learning opportunities associated with being a teacher. Sharing this information with others will not only serve to recruit people to the profession, but it will also hopefully remind you of why you became a teacher in the first place and the support mechanisms that are in place to help you stay focused on "making a difference in the lives of students."

Everyone needs support and appreciation for what we do. It gives us positive reinforcement about the job we are doing and helps us retain focus on the best aspects of the education business. This book is designed to provide another layer of support for beginning teachers by helping them to anticipate what to expect during the first year of teaching and beyond. It can certainly be helpful to any first-year teachers who read it but, in my opinion, the power of the publication lies in its potential to be a mentoring tool.

Use the ideas and questions posed throughout the work to begin discussions with new teachers at your school or district. Empower your new colleagues by talking through parent conferences and rehearsing Back-to-School Night presentations. Assist them in making the provided templates applicable for your school/district. Finally, any teacher can benefit from reflecting on the end of year questions provided, so use them to strengthen your practice as well as that of your colleagues. By collaborating as a team of language professionals, we should be able to better mentor our newest colleagues and retain them for years to come!

For more information on mentoring, visit www.actfl.org.

David Jahner, College Board

Acknowledgments

The author would like to express thanks to the following people and organizations who contributed to the Second Edition of this guide:

Winston-Salem/Forsyth County Schools, North Carolina

Some examples and pictures came from: Greg Williams, Sarah Kivett, Pat Hooker, Virginia Browne, Jennifer Solis, and Julia Figueroa Pagan

From the First Edition, thanks to:

Fairfax County Public Schools (VA)

Georgia Department of Education

National Association of District Supervisors of Foreign Languages (NADSFL)

Consortium for Assessing Performance Standards: A New Jersey FLAP Grant Project

Project Directors:

Jacqueline Gilbert, West Orange Public Schools

Mary Mackenzie, East Brunswick Public Schools

Martin Smith & Beatrice Yetman, Edison Public Schools

Carol Meulener & Rosanne Zeppieri, West Windsor-Plainsboro Public Schools

Ruth D. Chang

Lucrecia Chivukula

Susan Crooks

Greg Duncan

Yu He

David Jahner

Mimi Met

Laura Terrill

Please consult the Publications section of the ACTFL website (www.actfl.org) for information about:

World-Readiness Standards for Learning Languages

NCSSFL-ACTFL Can-Do Statements

Implementing Integrated Performance Assessment

All templates from this handbook can be downloaded from the Members section of the ACTFL website (www.actfl.org).